FoR
PAULA + Ea

with all good wishes
may you find your own
village if you have not
already done so. You
have great friends in Roxy
and John.

Peter Megargee Brown
Stonington Village
Connecticut

September 30, 1997.

Publication DAY

Village

Where to Live
and How to Live

ALSO BY PETER MEGARGEE BROWN

ONE WORLD AT A TIME
Tales of Murder, Joy and Love

RASCALS
The Selling of the Legal Profession

FLIGHTS OF MEMORY
Days Before Yesterday

THE ART OF QUESTIONING
Thirty Maxims

GUIDE SELECT GASTRONOMIQUE

Village

Where to Live and How to Live

PETER MEGARGEE BROWN

Foreword by Alexandra Stoddard

AN INDIGO BOOK
Benchmark Press
New York

Copyright © 1997 Peter Megargee Brown

All rights reserved. No reproduction of this book in whole or in part or in any form or sound may be made without written authorization of the copyright owner.
Published by BENCHMARK PRESS
1125 Park Avenue, Suite 6A
New York, New York 10128
Tel: (212) 289-5509
FAX: (212) 996-4625

Library of Congress Cataloging-in-Publication Data
Brown, Peter Megargee
VILLAGE: Where to Live and How to Live
Peter Megargee Brown—First Edition
ISBN 0-915011-06-10
Library of Congress Catalogue #95-83565
Manufactured in the United States of America
Editor, A. B. Stoddard
Cover Jacket Painting "Le Toit Orange"—Mougins, by Roger Mühl
—Alexandra Stoddard Collection
Book Jacket Photograph of Author in Claude Monet's Garden at Giverny
by Alexandra Stoddard
Jacket Design by Julia Estabrook Hoyt
Book Design by Marysarah Quinn and Mark Garofalo

1. Village
2. Cities
3. Suburbia
4. History and Development of Villages and Cities
5. Where to Live and How to Live—Philosophy
6. Biological Evolutionary Psychology Syndrome
7. Living Well in the New Millennium

Books also available by the author at *Benchmark Press:*
One World at a Time: Tales of Murder, Joy and Love
Rascals: The Selling of the Legal Profession
Flights of Memory: Days Before Yesterday
The Art of Questioning: Thirty Maxims

To purchase copies directly, call, fax or write *Benchmark Press*
1125 Park Avenue, Suite 6A
New York, New York 10128
Telephone: (212) 289-5509
Facsimile (FAX): (212) 996-4625

This is an INDIGO BOOK

Dedicated to

JOHN BOWEN COBURN

Table of Contents

Foreword

Village is far more than a book. Peter Brown has put his life and spirit into years of research, travel and contemplation to delve into the most pressing human issue, where and how to live. I've watched the author go through this exhilarating undertaking, reading hundreds of books and records, interviewing people of varied backgrounds and interests. Observing this process, I recall the words of Saint Catherine of Siena—"Heaven is on the way." This book became bigger than his preparation, more than words on a page: *Village* has a universality of its own.

Because Peter Brown has been a global observer for more than fifty years, he brings deep insights into his narrative. He takes the reader on a journey to all kinds of places, where he's lived as well as where he's traveled. Because he is a great writer, and a historian with a vivid memory, his innate curiosity as a philosopher makes *Village* a joy to read.

Village reflects firsthand experiences we can all share, beginning when we found our cottage in Stonington Village, Connecticut, in the summer of 1989. The author fell in love with village existence after spending most of his life in New York City, where his family had settled in 1927 on Carnegie Hill, described as a village within a city. This exciting passage from city to Water Street in southeastern Connecticut has transformed our lives.

Peter Brown's tribute to villages is reflective of his love of life. Village life, wherever in the world, has become an integral part of him—heart and soul. This appreciation, this joy in living, permeates every page as his words paint essays and moving stories.

The author is up-to-date on contemporary issues as well as general history, and his outlook on the world's complexities today is never cynical or pessimistic. He is able to take issues seriously with an optimistic attitude. *Village* is, over all, a very positive message, full of faith, hope and enthusiasm.

Peter Brown encourages us to feel we can create the spirit of the village, the place and the life inside our hearts, wherever we are, wherever we travel; we are connected to this mysterious, divine feeling when we are in the right place; we belong there, and the separation between our environment and ourselves melts away.

Village helps us find our own heaven within our possibilities and our dreams. Perhaps what we are all seeking, this inspired author eloquently points out, is here, right here, in a village, or similar place where we are, cultivating, as Voltaire said, our own garden—allowing us to slow down, walk about, observe, and feel content with both where we are and how we live.

ALEXANDRA STODDARD
Stonington Village,
Connecticut

Village

Where to Live
and How to Live

PART ONE

Wild Promise of the City

Over the great bridge, with the sunlight through the girders
making a constant flicker upon the moving cars, with the city
rising up across the river in white heaps and sugar
lumps…The city seen for the first time, in its first wild
promise of all the mystery and the beauty in the world…
"Anything can happen now that we've slid over this bridge," I
thought,
"anything at all …"

F. Scott Fitzgerald,
The Great Gatsby

I came to the City and it changed my life.

I was exalted by it, exulted in it. I was a young man at a great
personal threshold in a place and a moment throbbing with
possibility.

William Morris,
New York Days,
Upon his coming to New York City in 1967
to be editor-in-chief of Harper's magazine

I

I sought for the greatness and genius of America in her com-
modius harbors and her ample rivers, and it was not there; in
her fertile fields and boundless prairies, and it was not there; in
her rich mines and her vast world commerce, and it was not
there...America is great because she is good and if America
ever ceases to be good, America will cease to be great.

ALEXIS DE TOCQUEVILLE,
DEMOCRACY IN AMERICA

II

We think our civilization near its meridian, but we are yet
only at the cock-crowing and the morning star.

RALPH WALDO EMERSON,
POLITICS

III

Look to this day
For it is life,
The very life of life.
In its brief course lie all
The Realities and verities of existence,
The bliss of growth.

SANSKRIT PROVERB

I.
Village:
Image in the Mind

"Sweet Auburn! Loveliest village of the plain."

—OLIVER GOLDSMITH
THE DESERTED VILLAGE

This book of impressionistic essays tries to analyze one of humankind's deepest yearnings—*where* to live—and *how* to live. When Ralph Waldo Emerson, the last century's reflective philosopher, was changing his career after the death of his wife Ellen and his formal ministry, on returning from a European odyssey, he wrote in his journal, "I wish I knew *where* and *how* I ought to live."

This is the theme and search of our lives.

Let us begin with our thinking about the "village." As Socrates would say, before proceeding, let us first try to define "village." What is village in history, in our world, in America? The tomorrow we will soon be part of?

While the definition is difficult (because of variation and misnomer), there are some intangible nuances that we can grasp.

Remember in Sinclair Lewis' classic novel *Main Street* that Gopher Prairie, plainly a village, was called a "city" by its proud and upward mobile inhabitants. Outside of New England, citizens like to call their village a "town."

As to dimension, the space is small, somewhat nuclear, and houses and buildings, usually clustered, are *human-scale*. In a village the community is apt to be situated about an environmentally pleasing place (the kind of a site Native American Indians would naturally choose)—by the sea; overlooking a brisk river; perhaps with a view of a mountain or monumental rock; within a lovely valley such as Napa (California) or Mougins (France), Portofino or Positano (Italy); or on top of a precipice eagle-lookout to a sparkling bay; perhaps in fertile farm country with clean, neat painted barns, sturdy fences and horses, wagons and carriages (Lancaster, Pennsylvania); or the romantic villages of Île de Saint Barthélémy in the French Antilles, such as Gustavia and Guanahani on Grand Cul-de-Sac.

The village in our mind may develop and survive in the midst of a large city—Greenwich Village or Carnegie Hill, New York City, or Society Hill in Philadelphia.

In the countryside, the village may be a natural circle with a church or two, white and with exuberant steeple drawn from Hartford and from London, high, slim and seen for miles through elms, maples and oaks. Or churches with square-top towers, sometimes, as on Orange Street, Nantucket, with block-faced or oval clocks, chiming and bonging with golden hands; also black-green shutters on pure white clapboard houses, trimmed with pink geraniums, or purple, yellow and white pansies in window boxes, surrounded by white picket fences facing a village common dressed in lawns of spring Irish green and then rows along the roadside of May pink and white dogwood.

Villagers themselves are few to be seen except at festivals and special communal events. They have no saltwater taffy boardwalk, or nightclub as we know it. They cling to their rituals and customs as in Quimper, Brittany, but are also attentive to the serious business of sustaining themselves and their families.

The ancient redundant patterns of farming and fishing are now invisibly expanding to include cottage service industries, communicated long distances by high technology and swift transportation. Your office now can be where you are.

In most cases, true villagers appreciate how things are in the village and are less interested in commercial development, however camouflaged—high-rise buildings, billboards, casinos, supermarkets, glitz, neon, institutional housing projects, discos, bedlams and addict treatment centers of any kind. In this sense villagers are apt to be conservative. Traditionally and wrongfully, the city élites have tended to look down on villagers, treating them often from afar as, well, villains.

Villagers likely have internal amusements and gentle, outdoor games. For more complex, rougher and sophisticated entertainments, the villager may go away "to town," often a slice of suburbia on the outskirts of what would be called "the city."

As we approach even the smaller cities of the world, we see the spikes and sugar cubes of downtown skyscrapers. Today a palpable, mild, creeping rot has afflicted many downtown areas. The cities, large and small, are heroically and expensively engaged in resuscitation efforts often of no avail. The image of the villages, healthy, green and serene, may serve to inhibit the downtown rehabilitation.

It is perhaps ironic that those who have not lived anywhere but the village want to escape as soon as they can and go, like John Winthrop and hordes of others, to the City Set on the Hill. Often, all their dreams are encompassed in what they hope will someday come to pass in the city.

Those villagers who have happened to live in the city for a length of time know by heart its shortcomings, its ecstasies, its dangers and its disappointments. They are, in reverse, more content with their lot when living in the village and more often count their blessings—and say their prayers. The qualities of life are today, more than ever, unevenly distributed. The ex-urbanites in the village are happier perhaps because, having experienced the metropolis, they are more content with what they now have.

At the same time, city people transplanted to the village sometimes confound (and often irritate) the lifetime villagers by their avid appreciation, even wild enthusiasm, for simple pleasures such as a walk on a country road, a bicycle ride down Main Street, fishing off the dock, buying a baguette of bread and ordering fresh boiled lobster from Bill the fish man at the wharf (who asks if he can deliver it to the door). Often, real villagers find such behaviorial outbursts to be more than they can bear.

Everyone in the village knows everyone else—better than one would want to imagine. Pretense is no acceptable cover. Titles and past accomplishments, however hyped, are interesting, perhaps, but not persuasive if the character is weak and behavior unacceptable. Honesty reigns because many transactions are daily, eye to eye and on foot. The sword of respect is two-edged.

Everyone knows who you are in the village, which may cause some alarm to newcomers fresh from fancy places afar where they dwelled anonymously and solitarily in apartments apart from general humanity. This may cause the visitors expressed discomfort, or even some anxiety at what they archly call a "lack of privacy."

At the same time—because of the factor of size—the villagers as a whole are more aware of kindness, fairness and compassion toward others. They know, without bureaucratic government or institutional help, if someone is in need and how assistance can be offered quietly and arranged in a fruitful, dignified way.

Villages so defined, I would venture, provide more sense of fair dealing, friendship and democratic behavior, even simple justice, than other bigger kinds of towns, suburbia or modern megacities. The human scale of the village naturally lends an aura of generous relations. We are, after all, the same biological yearning souls of the Late Stone Age, 20,000 to 30,000 years ago.

In the real village, social and economic class lines (meaning exclusion) are apt to dissolve and be replaced by a sounder, more rewarding community with increased sincere collegiality. People of different interests and varied background experiences seem to thrive better (and cope better) in the village. And to the extent to which we can measure, they appear to be happier overall.

2.

Finding the Village: The Day the Village House Was Discovered

"Teach us delight in simple things."

—RUDYARD KIPLING
THE CHILDREN'S SONG

Stonington Village on the shore of southeastern Connecticut may be an example of an American village that developed courageously, with increasing charm and dignity, despite two invasions, economic downturns and critical wars at home and abroad over a period of three centuries.

We often forget who introduces us to good fortune. We rarely forget who presents us with grief. In the case of Stonington Village in New England, it was a coincidence of good fortune. Here's how it happened:

Daughter Alexandra chose Connecticut College across from the Coast Guard Academy in New London. In three years there she and her friends would drive twenty minutes over the Thames River to a slim peninsula called Stonington Village pointing south toward

Watch Hill, Rhode Island. On the west side is the Stonington Village harbor; on the east, Little Narragansett Bay; directly out beyond the breakwaters, is Block Island Sound, and then the Atlantic Ocean and the Azores. Since Stonington Village is essentially a sliver of a peninsula separated from the rest of the mainland by the shore rail line, the village glows with the character of an island at sea.

The primary draw for young Alexandra and her friends was first a restaurant called Noah's on Water Street owned by John and Dorothy Papp. John has been president of the Village Improvement Society with a litany of good works in the village while Dorothy has been elected warden (mayor) of the Stonington Borough (called Stonington Village). Here in cozy delight Alexandra and her friends would enjoy a country breakfast at Noah's and often lunch as well. Here they would hang out.

The village stores and several restaurants (Kitchen Little, now Walter and Stephanie's eclectic-cuisine Water Street Café; Harbour View; and for seafood, Skipper's Dock) occupy several diminutive blocks on Water Street. The street has dashes of residential and then commercial zoning on the way south down to the Point. For the most part these two-to-three story buildings in the village nucleus are 19th century, clapboard and old brick.

Alexandra liked to walk and talk down Water Street a quarter mile to the south tip of the village peninsula. There is a 300-degree view of the Stonington Village harbor, Fishers Island Sound, Long Island Sound, Block Island Sound, Watch Hill over in Rhode Island with a golden dome of a Victorian hotel, Little Narragansett Bay with small islands and classic Currier & Ives white and yellow houses along the shore.

Main Street, paralleling Water Street, overlooks the bay to the east and handsomely features most of the dozen 18th-century houses in

Stonington Village. Young Alexandra's walking tour would be circular: down Water Street to a mild commercial zone, now mostly antique shops, near Harbour View restaurant, which adjoins a sturdy 500-foot pier housing, as noted, the sister restaurant Skipper's Dock, where sturdy laughing gulls can share your lobster and fried clams, with haughty aplomb.

Up from Skipper's is Cannon Square, suddenly, commemorating the second repulsion of attacking British ships in August, 1814. Two cannons that performed much of the repulsing are displayed on the small square common facing the Point where the first invasion in August, 1775 (to gather food for beleaguered Boston Redcoats), was aggressively, if unsuccessfully, attempted.

Each Fourth of July the whole village, in suitable costume, celebrates the day with fife and drum, a lively parade, historic readings and salutes in Cannon Square. King George III is given his due.

Farther down Water Street are the old red brick and gray stone factories that have a long history of desultory manufacture, now dormant. A Japanese entrepreneur one day in the late 1980s acquired the plant (and presumed water rights) for $10 million, with an eye to building condominiums and marinas, arguably in one of the world's most beautiful settings of sea and land—overlooking three states: New York, Rhode Island and Connecticut.

The villagers were not pleased with the prospect to convert the property of a thin-reeded, quiet community into more lively endeavors, with their attendant traffic and commotion. They formed a resistance committee, like militia, of great vitality and clout. Handbills prepared by committee with regular updates led by eager volunteers were delivered to supporters by hand. There was a suggestion of the Minutemen on the Lexington Green in April, 1775.

In a few months the villagers succeeded in defeating the innovative if disproportionate commercial plan that would have, as they say, altered the neighborhood.

After a visit to DuBois Beach, a small sandy enclave to the right at Stonington Point, among great Brittany rocks, where children play and adults swim lazily to the float, daughter Alexandra would then swing around to head back by the Old Lighthouse, now a museum, run with enthusiasm by the Stonington Historical Society. Climbing the stairs of the Gothic stone lighthouse into the glass signal chamber gives the visitor a panorama of a great spirit of place, all in proper proportion and scale—gable-roofed houses, sailboats large and small, motorboats, a ferry now and then, the fishing fleet draggers, schooners and shadowy tankers, far out, coming and going from mysterious ports of call.

A successor lighthouse is seen in the distance near Fishers Island, blinking its warning of dangerous submerged rocks close to the entrance to the old Stonington Harbor.

The sun sets in glory over there and, as autumn approaches, moves over westward in extraordinary hues of yellow, purple, orange, umber and green. At the entrance of Stonington Village harbor, through the 1825 breakwater, the melancholic foghorn intermittently rises and falls, whether the weather is inclement or not. (Night and day we grow to depend on its audible breathing.) The blazing sunset excites dive-bombing gulls that swerve, laugh and cry through the radiance until the sun sinks down and shadows creep across the sky.

Young Alexandra goes across to the beginning, or end, of Main Street by the yellow and white mid-19th-century Gurdon Trumbull house, its lawns flowing down to Little Narraganset Bay. To its right is a fine flower and vegetable garden planted and tended by Harry Fowler. It was Harry and Emily Fowler who welcomed us to the village and invited us to lunch with a real estate agent on their wood terrace overlooking Harry's garden and the Bay.

Down Main Street there continue an array of 18th- and 19th-century houses in native stone, white, yellow and gray clapboard, well groomed and proud in the afternoon light. Not much in architecture changed in Nantucket after oil was discovered in Pennsylvania, displacing its precious prize of whale oil. Not much has changed in Stonington Village either after the steamboats stopped their rounds to New York (with well-heeled passengers and fancy steamer trunks), after railroad bridges were built along the Connecticut shoreline to New York City.

Main Street lifts northward to High Street where we see Wadawanuck Square, the major common of Stonington Village, also bordered by attractive houses. At the center used to be the old Wadawanuck Hotel, built to serve the railroad passengers, visited they say by the Astors and the Vanderbilts when the Boston Providence railroad was brought to the Village Common by the famed artist James Whistler's father. From there, after a night's conviviality and rest, the steamboats would take the passengers and their fashionable belongings to New York City. This exciting activity, before suitable bridges were built across the broad Connecticut rivers, brought great prosperity and incipient style to Stonington Village, implanting a grace and beauty that remains today.

The Whistler railroad, like a stage set, terminated adjacent to the white Second Congregational Church on Main Street with its square black-faced clock tower. From here we are regularly tolled by hourly striking bongs and by its resonant bells on Sunday mornings, a heartening sound, pure and instructive. On the northeast corner of the Common is the pristine Saint Mary's Church, with a graceful steeple that speaks of old New England; next to that is the current day meeting house, the U.S. Post Office, where villagers gossip and exchange information; and in the Common itself, replacing in 1899 the burned-down hotel, is the proportioned, scaled Stonington Free Library—light, airy, helpful with plenty of comfortable room to read, write or browse.

On the south end of the Common is the Book Mart, more than a hundred and fifty years of book selling in a gentle advisory way: "Here, Mrs. Harris, you might be interested in this new one by Edith Wharton, who summers, you know, in Newport on the West End…"

By now young Alexandra has made somewhat of a circle. She can stand on High Street and Water Street looking south toward the Point, observe all of the village center from this vantage and glimpse the Village Dock, where resplendent bishops annually bless the fishing fleet. Down the way, sailors from all over America come in to Dodson's Boat Yard for solace, fuel, food and repairs.

In sight we can see, or imagine we can see, to the second story meeting room where in April, 1775, Reverend John Rathbone gathered the first congregation in the village. You can step into Studio 33, the village frame shop at the left, to see the first Rathbone-led village Baptist church foundations, still there after a fire took away the rest.

At Water Street and Pearl walking south, Alexandra would stop by the green-painted brick News Office (the oldest establishment in the village) run by Frankie Keane, who has lived and sold newspapers, magazines and sundries as long as anyone can remember. His memory of the old days is perceptive and colored with gentle ironic observation. Alexandra would buy *The (New London) Day* and *The*

New York Times and a pack of Doublemint gum, and, evading Mr. Buck's red MG roadster, she would cross back and forth, looking into the myriad stores.

She might negotiate a haircut from Doug the village barber on a Saturday and wheedle sandwiches and cookies from the Village Market for the following week at college. These zigzag visits would include visits to antique shops. All of this activity within a few yards—on foot. Soon, starved on this Sunday, she could be back at Noah's. The chefs are John and Stanley, who met in military service in Europe. After deciding to open a restaurant someday in an ideal location, they found Stonington Village and have been happy with their discovery ever since. (Alexandra and I have a saying from time to time: if we ever get to Heaven, we will remember to ask Saint Peter, "Who is cooking tonight? John or Stanley?")

When we would come up to New London to see Alexandra she would whisk us over to Stonington Village for a walk around and lunch. One time as we walked down Main Street, the mother Alexandra stopped at the corner of Wall Street to look at the picturesque houses in the village, the white picket fences, the flowering trees and sparkling water views visible on both sides of the peninsula and boats going by.

"You know, Alexandra, I think we want to buy an 18th- century house, in really wreck condition, that we can afford, with possibilites of restoration and unquestionably a peek or two at the water, since we've come so far. What do you think?"

Young Alexandra laughed, and could only respond, "Oh, Mom." Nothing more was said, and we moved along Main Street, admiring the Oliver Smith (1761) house, now Mitchell, on the east side, with perfect symmetry, a center chimney and a large picketed yard with apple trees readying to burst in bloom. (In 1775 Captain Oliver Smith was in charge of village soldiers who drove off the first British marauders at the Point. He was promoted to major, then colonel and died peacefully a hero in this handsome house.)

But Alexandra's mother was serious. As graduation at Connecticut College approached, we made plans to spend a weekend searching for a house in the village.

When we arrived that spring weekend in Stonington Village, we decided to park the car on the harbor side of Water Street near a house painted cornflower blue (plaque says C. BREED 1760); it had been architecturally expanded, still blue, to fan out at the water's edge. The front door is tangerine.

Across Water Street, Alexandra suddenly noticed an extremely plain house, painted dreary brown taupe. It had an ill-suited entrance with Carvel ice-cream cone drops and silly stick pillars; no picket fence; no shutters; no window boxes; and a lone hung window at the gable. No love. What attracted Alexandra's eye was a "For Sale" sign in the window and the name of the broker. There was no sign of life, inside or out. Here was, for the neighborhood, an incongruous hovel. On the left of the front door was a washed-out plaque (installed by the Stonington Historical Society some years past) that read:

REV. JOHN RATHBONE
1775

As Alexandra crossed Water Street she turned to say, "Well, that's one requirement." She then tiptoed up to the left front window and looked in. What she saw that May spring day made her smile, for the inside view brought back memories of a childhood house on the Post Road in Weston, Massachusetts, outside Boston: the Drivers Farm.

It was the high-noon piercing sun in the south windows of this house that stunned her. The light illuminated the wide golden pine floorboards. As far as one could see into the house there were these old floors without any covering. The space was unfurnished, musty and dusty, but the fireplace mantels, bookcases and arches were generous and well carved.

That was it. "Peter, I think we should see this house. Somehow I like the *bones*." I said, "Well, we'll see. But now we should go over to Cannon Square for lunch."

We were welcomed at the Fowlers' and led to their guest house across the garden to the south. This handsome little house is both charming and comfortable, built by a local ropemaker in 1780. At lunch, when the real estate agent arrived, we told her of Alexandra's advance look at the taupe house across from the blue house on Water Street. "Oh," she said, "that house is *not* on my list. I have some other prospects to show you this afternoon."

So we drove around the village for several hours looking at houses that did not seem to ignite Alexandra's ardor, or mine either. This was disappointing.

Alexandra was thinking of the first house she had spied. "Can't you make it possible for us to see the house that's for sale on Water Street?" "Well," the agent replied, "maybe it's possible. It's with another broker, you know." Alexandra said: "Well, whether it is or not, I'd like to see it. I'm sure you can work it out."

The next day we received word that the house would be opened and shown to us. We went through the rooms, as the new agent told us that an itinerant Baptist minister, John Rathbone, decided to settle down with his family here in the village that was then called Stonington Long Point. He had persuaded a group of friendly church carpenters to build a house for him in 1775—the year he gathered the first Baptist congregation at Water Street and Pearl—"the year *before* the Revolution," the agent said, with emphasis.

The house in 1775 had two stories, five fireplaces (winters were cold) and no gable roof. In 1808 the village doctor William Hyde married the village belle Rhoda Palmer; a few years later, bought the house from the Rathbone family.

The Hydes lived in the house until he died in 1873 and she in 1877. After that, we were told, various occupants came and went. The property, while unusually firm of foundation (with a large, dry, stone-lined cellar) and on relatively high land, was neglected, sometimes abandoned, and became increasingly run down.

In the early 20th century the Rathbone-Hyde property was surrounded by other village houses. The shore side of Water Street now also became lined with houses, evidently ignoring the historic prospect of frequent hurricanes. The trade and prosperity of the 19th century gradually subsided as railroads took away businesses to New London, New Haven, Hartford and New York. The steamships, so colorful and romantic, were retired. The pace of trade simmered down. Left behind was a quiet serene village.

Our walk around the old Rathbone house showed that Alexandra was right: the house had good bones. Yet the charm was hard to find because entrepreneurs in the early 1980s had purchased the house from the struggling landlady who ran it as a rooming house for many years. Each tenant had an assigned space, sealed off from others by lock and key; each had his or her own hot plate; three entries and exits were employed. The overall effect was painfully dreary, reclusive and sad.

The neighbors' reaction to this ugly decline was not to protest but rather simply to ignore the site. Even when the Stonington Historical Society in an earnest little ceremony put up the plaque "Rev. John Rathbone–1775," the accolade did not succeed in breaking the icy presence of so forlorn a Cinderella among fashionable sisters on all sides.

We were told that the entrepreneurs may have added insult by conceiving a selling strategy of fast-stain cosmetics that left the house unwanted and unsold for several years despite, out of curiosity, most of the villagers, many with white gloves, having trooped through when the "For Sale" sign went up in the mid 1980s. No one seemed to want this orphan.

Alexandra by this time had been designing houses for almost thirty years. As a child she had lived in a series of 18th-century houses. It occurred to her that what turned potential buyers off were the incredible color choice of taupe on the exterior of the house, the unbelievable dead cockroach tones of yellow, green and blue splashed over the woodwork, closets, doors, mantels. The effect was horrible—absolutely repulsive.

Despite these indignities, Alexandra could see beyond, without reconstruction and fancy conceits, to a white white house, with bottle-green shutters, an antique fan window at the attic gable to replace the double-hung window, removal of the spindly 19th-century entrance with its thin plywood door and replacement with a period white hand-carved door frame with panels, a concave molding and fanlight window and a larger heavy door on solid brass hinges.

Her prescience kept her from fleeing out of the house with me following. Instead, she told the patient agent that she'd like to look outside. As we had moved about the small rooms of the house, the sun shone in through budding maple trees. We agreed that even though the Rathbone house was now surrounded in the middle of a tiny village, it had highly unusual light that seemed to come bouncing into it from all directions. As we came to learn, this light was empowered from morning until sunset by the waves and ripples of the Bay, the ocean, the sound and the harbor. The sun was sparkled, struck with fire-like diamonds, repeatedly ricocheting from the sea into the depths of the house. We came to call it the house of light.

We were led in this bright sunshine through the front door around to a small gray stone path to the rear of the house, where we saw a yard of moldy grass and dank flagstone, a motley picket fence to the south, a high beige-white wooden fence to the east. No flowers, potted or grounded. The scene was dismal despite the brightness of the day.

At that point, when I was ready to move on, Alexandra exclaimed, "Look!" She raised an arm to an ancient lilac tree in full bloom in the corner of the yard. Situated in front of us, to our right, were, as it turned out, several lilac trees entwined and blossoming together in high dudgeon. Some of the lilac blossoms were purple; an equal number, rising some 18 feet, were white. The combination of such unexpected beauty caused us to stare and stand back, breathless. This moment of revelation moved us both as if we had been subjected to some sort of omen.

Even the real estate agent, grown discouraged by our comments, perked up with unexpected delight. We all felt the impact of what this village house had conjured up for us at this moment. As we glanced back at the vista of the flowering lilac tree against the blue sky, we felt a mystical rush of appreciation; we thought we heard the singing of birds and a promise of golden bliss and serenity. We had discovered the village house.

3.

Origin of "The Lilac Tree, the Singing and the Gold"

I like what a psychic California friend told me one day—that there is no such thing as a coincidence.

In 1940, entering freshman year at Yale, our Class of 1944 was assigned, in our mandatory English class, a short story, "The Apple Tree," by John Galsworthy, published in 1918 by Charles Scribner's Sons. This was a touching love story that impacted on my classmates to a greater extent than anyone would believe…

Two English lads, the story goes, just out of the university go on a walking trip together in the countryside in the springtime. They chance to meet a pretty charismatic seventeen-year-old maiden named Megan, with slim waist, full dark hair, limpid gray-blue eyes and long lashes, as I recollect. Both are instantly charmed by Megan. But one, Frank Ashurst, through engaging circumstances, is smitten, pure innocent first love, while at Megan's aunt's old rural farm, under the large apple tree in the orchard, near the flowing stream. A memorable scene is drawn by Galsworthy, conducive to deep romance, with flowers coming up all over and birds singing their hearts out.

Frank, after a few days of romance, makes the wavering choice to go back to London alone without the awkward pain of saying good-bye to Megan, by now devoted to him. Of course he regrets the decision all his humdrum life and, on the silver anniversary of his marriage to a sister of a classmate at Rugby, by coincidence, on their wandering celebratory motor trip, he suddenly discovers he is picnicking exactly where he and his classmate met the unforgettable village maid, along a country road in Devonshire, 26 years before.

Found among Galsworthy's literary papers, penciled in a notebook, was a poem prompted by Galsworthy's own encounter with a young lady during a "walking trip in Wales in 1904." His sole companion on that tour says in his introduction to the *Letters of John Galsworthy*:

> In a lonely wild tract we met a lovely girl, who, passing us…was too modest to look in our faces but kept her eyes shyly on the ground. From this incident sprang "The Apple Tree," one of Galsworthy's finest stories.

CLUE #1
Galsworthy's unpublished poem "The Apple Tree" is just six lines long:

> He thought :"Those rocks old memories bring;
> Yes, surely, 'tis the same!"
> Once more, to his remembering,
> Over the hill she came,

Modest and pretty as the spring;
And Megan was her name!

CLUE #2

On the first page of his short story, Galsworthy reveals in an epigraph the source of his title and his theme—the rhapsody and poignancy of first young love:

The apple tree, the singing, and the gold

EURIPIDES
HIPPOLYTUS
(translation of Sir Gilbert Murray)

CLUE #3

The Galsworthy 91-page love story describes the young man's sensuous romance with Megan as much with *lilacs* as with *apple blossoms*. Galsworthy was evidently much intoxicated with lilacs, their mysterious color, the simple beauty of a spray of lilac in the orchard, the rapture of a single lilac blossom and "the scent of lilacs [filling] the air."

These coincidences perhaps, of time and place and scent, wholly enveloped us that May spring day in Stonington Village in the back yard of that otherwise forlorn house. I knew then, and coincidentally Alexandra did as well, that we must live in this house *with* the lilac tree.

4.

Birth of
Stonington Village

"History is the essence of innumerable biographies."

THOMAS CARLYLE

Every village has a history, often forgotten, usually influenced by the actions of certain strong personalities facing turbulent events, not so pervasive and overwhelming to human and environmental challenges, as historian Arnold Joseph Toynbee would say, as to snuff out the spirit of the place.

Residents and a few historians share appreciation of the origins of this idyllic peninsula village stuck out into a widening circle of harbor, sounds, bays and ocean; rock-ribbed lighthouses, old breakwaters, offshore sand and scrub islands, one divided into minuscule slivers of the states of New York, Connecticut and Rhode Island (where in Prohibition days bootleggers nimbly juggled booze depending on which state's cutter was raiding); and always the melodious flow of sailboats on the cobalt horizon.

Stonington peninsula village has been a fishing village of sorts for three hundred years and more. The 25-boat fishing fleet today comes in and goes out through the narrow inlet to and from the Village

Dock. The fleet used to dock closer to the Point, behind the 1825 breakwater. But the 1938 hurricane wiped out the breakwater—and now the fishing fleet has retreated farther into the harbor for protection.

The lineage of the intrepid fishermen is Portuguese, largely from the Azores; their solace is the Holy Ghost Society, an oasis of a building on Main Street that shares our east side high white fence. This is the venerable former Nicholas Palmer mansion of the 19th century, now a social club of vitality and umpa-pa band music, ample food and family conviviality. Life's frustrations and memories of stormy seas can be soothed. We throw open our windows, break out a bottle of wine with friends and join in the fun of village life.

The laughing gulls closely hail and inhale the arrival of the fishing boats returning chock-full of varieties of the world's freshest fish. Lobster boats slip in and drop their catch at the Point next to Skippers Dock. Pleasure boats large and small take up the rhythm and the beat of holiday times in summery seasons. All is well.

This uncommon panorama of gentle activity displays, surprisingly, 350 years of rich American history—and, as in Concord, Cambridge, Granville and Sudbury, provides some keys to the development of sensible democracy, wisdom and happiness in New England and beyond.

Paradoxes and unexpected heroic events enliven the history of Stonington Village, and many of them are unknown. Holland first claimed the Stonington area based on the discoveries of Henry Hudson, an Englishman and agent of the Dutch East India Company. By 1614 Captain Adrian Block under the Dutch flag had explored—six years before the Pilgrims landed the *Mayflower* at Plymouth—the Stonington region for the Dutch East India Company in his minute sloop *The Restless,* and had sailed 75 miles up the Connecticut River, one of the most beautiful in the colony. Block also surveyed the Stonington Village area at this early time carefully noting his findings in his ship's log. The fertile Connecticut River valley soon became one of the colony's most populous areas. Attractive Block Island in the ocean off Rhode Island was given the explorer's name. (He also explored and logged the New Jersey coast, observing and mapping what are now Bay Head, Mantoloking and Barnegat Bay.)

The green, handsome jewel of Block Island is sandy beached and today a village haven for summer visitors who arrive on bird-like airplanes, sailboats and ferries from shore ports. A few hardy souls hibernate throughout the winter months waiting for the first crocus.

In 1636 the Reverend Thomas Hooker took a devout group from Massachusetts overland, by what would become Sudbury, to Hartford, Connecticut, the first English settlement in this region. They had turned from the Puritan ways to worship in the Baptist tradition. (The earliest Baptist church in Hartford has a high and airy spire that was happily "borrowed" when the new Saint Mary's Church was built on the common in Stonington Village in 1955.)

In 1638 a few Puritans from Massachusetts Bay led by Jonathan Davenport settled in a garden-like region overlooking Long Island Sound, backed dramatically by huge West Rock. This area was named Quinnipiac by the Indians before being given the name New Haven. Here is the final ground of wordsmith Noah Webster, Eli Whitney of cotton gin fame and Roger Sherman, signer of the Declaration of Independence. Turncoat Benedict Arnold also lived here with his family after leaving his birthplace at Norwich, Connecticut, up the Thames from New London.

Here, too, Elihu Yale gave a number of books to a struggling Congregational educational endeavor that graciously took his name. The rector of the First Congregational Church in Stonington, Reverend Albert Noyes, a trustee of Yale before it was finally settled in New Haven, donated his library, but I know of no buildings named after him.

Connecticut was inhabited by a strong flow of emigrants from the Massachusetts Bay Colony, who were motivated by rich available land in the Connecticut River valley and energized, too, by moral fervor. Here they hoped to live and worship as they thought necessary to their religious beliefs.

The early Stonington region before European migration was a hunting and fishing turf of the warlike Pequot Indians of Iroquois race. The Pequots' strong sense of pride and spirit of place and love of tribal ritual gave them a special preference for the Stonington peninsula—or Point (later Village and Borough)—a favored place for their smoking wigwams overlooking the harbor, Fishers Island, Watch Hill, Rhode Island and Little Narragansett Bay. That Indians loved this place first is a badge for its panorama of rare beauty.

In this environment of serenity and brilliant sunsets there were easy clamming, fishing, and lobstering as well as opportunity to capture rabbits, squirrels, wolves and bears in the forest. These activities subsequently formed the basis for the early trading posts up the Thames River and the Pawcatuck River into Rhode Island.

Across the water, in Rhode Island and along Long Island, lived another Indian tribe with a reputation for dignity and bravery—the Narragansetts. They may have made the critical difference whether the English would be able to continue to exist in this part of the colony: As early as 1630, when the Pequots conspired to a grand plan to kill every colonial settler, the chief sachem of the Narragansetts was urged to join in this plan to "sweep the English into the sea." But the sachem refused the invitation to join forces with the Pequots in the plot to annihilate the white settlers. Word of the grand plan leaked out; the small clusters of colonists were put on alert. Within months the Pequots attacked the Narragansetts to subjugate them and then, together, turn on the English.★

After savage forays back and forth, the Connecticut community with help from Boston Puritans organized a small vigilante force under Captain John Mason of the Mystic-New London area. He cannily allied his army with the Mohegan Indians under their brave chief, Uncas. The first attack was to be against the fortified village of the Pequots on Mystic Hill, up the Pequot River (now the Thames). More than 700 Pequots stood behind the fort over a palisade—huge trees driven in the ground, with space for Pequot arrows to fly. The wigwams were in the rear of their fort.

On May 10, 1637, Captain Mason and the Mohegans set off down the Connecticut River. After several days, Mason and his army with his Indian colleagues started the journey across country to the Pequot stronghold. The Pequots believed the Mason attackers would first come up the Pequot River on the palisade side. When their scouts reported that the army had passed by the Pequot fort, they turned to celebration in the mistaken notion that the Mason party was afraid to engage the mighty Pequot fortress.

Before daybreak, Captain Mason moved up the hill with fewer than 600 men. At this point Mason switched his strategy from an attack solely from the river side to the east to attack from both sides. Aware that they were outnumbered—facing more than 700

★See *Stonington Chronology, 1649-1949* by William Haynes (Higginson Book Co., Salem, Mass. 1949) and *The Fine Old Town of Stonington* by Katherine B. Crandall (Book and Tackle Shop 1994).

Pequots—they set fire to the huts and wigwams on the north. The fire sweeping through the fort decided the outcome, a devastating and, some say, permanent Pequot defeat.

After the Pequots were subdued and their plan of annihilation crushed, settlers by the hundreds again flooded into the Connecticut River valley—the most fertile, navigable and beautiful valley along the colonial coast. Pilgrim Governor John Winthrop's son, also named John, arrived in 1645 from the Massachusetts Bay Colony to encourage settlers to move to the New London area (formerly called Pequot). John Winthrop, the younger, was in fact the catalyst for Stonington's birth since he brought William Chesebrough of the Plymouth Colony to assist him in recruiting settlers from Massachusetts. Chesebrough had come from England to Boston in 1630 with the elder John Winthrop, who was earnestly seeking, along with Peter Buckeley, the elusive "City Set on the Hill."

Chesebrough, traveling home from New London to Massachusetts through the forest along the Stonington shore, discovered a beautiful small saltwater cove on the west bank of Wequetequock River, now within Stonington town. He noted the plentiful fish, shellfish and wild game as well as the idyllic land and seascape. He made his choice and became the first white settler in the Stonington area. To this sheltered cove he brought his wife and four sons, becoming a respected trader with the Indians because of his acquired skills of gunsmith and blacksmith.

How did this region acquire the name "Stonington"? With no certainty, I'm inclined to the lament of a pioneer farmer near Chesebrough's place who complained of the innumerable stones he had to plow up and drag away before he could plant. Today we see backbreakingly laid-out dry rock walls all across this countryside.

The first person to join William Chesebrough at the new trading settlement directly north of the present Stonington Village was Thomas Stanton, who became equally prominent in the region; he was an energetic trader and community leader. He received exclusive license from the General Court to trade with the Indians in this region.

Stanton built a trading post in 1651 and later a home on the banks of the Pawcatuck River, in 1657, where his family joined him. There is a marker near the bend of the river indicating the site of the house of Thomas Stanton "the Indian interpreter—1651." In fact, so adept was Stanton with intricate dialects that he was appointed interpretor general of the New England colonies. He is also remembered as the local representative of the General Court of Connecticut and a founder of the first church in Stonington, the First Congregational called the Old Road Church on Agreement Hill. Subsequently, he became one of the first judges in New London County.

Thomas Stanton's characterization on the town founders' monument in the Wequetequock cemetery says, "A man of widespread and lasting importance to the colonies, and identified with nearly every transaction between the natives and colonists up to the year of his death."

Another significant settler in Stonington was Thomas Minor, the noted diarist, who came from England first to New Salem in 1630 and then to Stonington 22 years later, where he built his house across from William Chesebrough's on the west shore of Wequetequock Cove.

After Thomas Minor sold his house to one of the founders of

Stonington, Walter Palmer, for 100 pounds and a few cows, he built a new house for his family in Quiambaug—between Stonington Village and Mystic to the west. Minor was soon joined in this new hamlet near the Mystic River by Captain John Gallup and Captain George Denison and their families. Denison had been trained with Cromwell's army in England and rose, before wounds relieved him from duty, to the rank of colonel of cavalry. Nine generations of Denisons have lived in a 1717 house in Quiambaug on the site of the original house. The Minor family (with the name changed to Miner) have continued to live in this region as well. Connecticut climate, I have often heard, encourages longevity and creativity.

The early settlers at Wequetequock Cove and Quiambaug were subjected to conflicting territorial claims of Connecticut and Massachusetts. These disconcerting disputes left the settlers in a limbo of having no assurance of security from the administration of either General Court. The settlers were constantly under attack and siege by various bands of hostile Indians. Frustrated by failure to respond to their need for protection, the settlers in 1658 issued a declaration of independence calling themselves "The Association of Poquatuck People." This independent spirit appeared again and again, particularly in 1775, 1776 and 1812–14.

By the end of the 1660s fifty families had settled in Stonington in the area of (1) Pawcatuck and the Cove (2) Mystic and (3) around the area to the north of Stonington Village where the Old Road Church, First Congregational Church, stands today.

In 1669 Thomas Stanton and his committee planned Stonington's first highway (four feet wide) following the early route known as the Pequot Trail. It subsequently became known as the Post Road (Route 1). This is, by way of continuity, the same Post

Road that passes by Manhattan's Carnegie Hill, now called Third Avenue.

The Stonington peninsula would soon develop naturally into a maritime village of both vitality and charm.

5.

A Maritime Village with Great Charm

Although the larger Town of Stonington was chartered in 1649, the village area on the peninsula remained a cattle pasture until a century later, when in 1752 Edward and John Denison purchased a three-acre lot on Stonington Long Point from Elihu Chesebrough.

These children of original settlers were engaged in varied maritime activities along the Pawcatuck River and made the first move to introduce people, houses and seaport business to the barren peninsula. Here was the simple beginning of the slow mercurial development of Stonington Village.

Soon roads were built from the Point to Mystic, Westerly and Preston. A decade later there were forty buildings on the Point and 35 families living there. By the start of the Revolution, eighty families (about 500 people) resided there, occupied with coastwise fishing, shore whaling, commerce and incipient lucrative West Indies trade, including all the sundry activities in support of maritime ocean shipping. Stringent British blockades during the Revolutionary War slowed this development throughout the New England coastal area.

By the first years of the 19th century, the so-called Stonington Long Point settlers restored and expanded the maritime activities, heartened that the British were entangled in diverting hostilities with the French. Now there were more than 150 buildings on the Point, demonstrating an energetic confidence in the future.

Stonington Point leaders then petitioned the Connecticut Legislature to become more independent of Stonington Town and to handle their own affairs as Stonington Borough—ironically in the efficient English style of local government, emulating old Sudbury borough in Suffolk, England. The petition was granted, and a new chapter took place for the small peninsula that was still ambiguously called Stonington Long Point, Stonington Village or Stonington Borough. Stonington Borough has managed well over the years as a governing unit and now is the oldest in Connecticut.

After the War of 1812 ended in 1814, the Village of Stonington enjoyed exponential shipping, whaling, sealing, fishing and related maritime activities up to the commencement of the bloody four-year Civil War in 1861.

The quintessential charm of Stonington Village may be accounted for in part by the fact that the village by 1880 had acquired the look, size and the special ambience that it has today. For more than a century the change of appearance has been minimal. The village remains surrealistically a sliver of the 18th and 19th centuries even as we enter the 21st century. Walking through the village, we are moved by the extraordinarily well preserved character and harmony of the whole peninsula village.

This delightful time-warp illusion is heightened by such critical ingredients, rare in America, as the human-scale, intimate, clustered houses of eclectic yet compatible design and fabric; only two streets paralleling the harbor on the west and Little Narraganset Bay on the east, with just a few small streets crossing the narrow width of the peninsula; the Village finger of land, pointing to the ocean (where waves are sometimes visible crashing on the outer breakwaters) being slim enough to inhibit obnoxious developments of factories, housing projects, heavy commercial and shipyard enterprises that would bring pollution waste, noise and congestion. Geography in this way plays a saving grace; and the character and foresight of the settlers of Stonington Village, their innate sense of aesthetics, energy and care, served to preserve an especially attractive place for later generations to enjoy, somehow impervious to the lures of the carnival and the boardwalk, neon and honky-tonk, tinsel and casino. Sound leadership with strong resident participation, ever vigilant, accounts for a unique heritage—worth protecting, many believe, at all costs.

6.

Stonington Village
A Little Research
Can Be Rewarding

One summer day in 1989 Alexandra and I were painting the entrance hallway of our house on Water Street, with the front door open.

A scholarly lady from the Stonington Historical Society came by on her way south to the Old Lighthouse Museum down at the Point. She glanced at us with our paintbrushes and overalls, then at the plaque on the front clapboard of the house:

REV. JOHN RATHBONE—1775

She hesitated at the door and then, looking up, said: "Hello. Welcome to the Village...[pause] Do you know that your house is *not* the Rathbone house. You are in the *Hyde* house—so-called after the village doctor William Hyde who lived here for many years until his death. Down at the Lighthouse Museum we have a lot of his medical instruments and memorabilia. He was a blood letter, you know...," she mysteriously tossed off to us as she moved south down Water Street.

This sudden exclamation of historical trivia somehow agitated me as I continued to paint, yet her words had aroused my curiosity. Particularly, when I recalled that at the recent annual Fourth of July Village Parade, a volunteer executive of the Stonington Historical Society, although smiling, had pointedly said to me: "If you think your house was built in 1775, then *you* prove it."

Perhaps outside of New England one would wonder, who cares? What difference does it make? But here in these parts there seems to be a clinging if not cloying concern for historical fact and priority— even if only within a purview of 300 years.

Possibly, I had already caught this infectious predilection, for there and then I started, somewhat aimlessly, looking up the record that remains to see what fragmentary enlightenment could be found. Nothing tedious or arcane, but merely a look around in the Stonington Free Library, some Historical Society records and maybe ten books Margaret Davol kindly had identified for me from the cache at her village Book Mart.

My amateur inquiry of origins of the "Rathbone-Hyde" house has taken five years or so, off and on—a sort of engaging puzzle game where pieces were put together, sometimes haphazardly and often inaccurately. At the same time, as I pursued the chase, it became surprisingly more fun than chore.

Here's briefly what I found out:

Reverend John Rathbone (or Rathbun) lived and preached in Stonington Long Point (the village) as early as 1772, according to the travel journals of Isaac Backus, a Baptist historian and itinerant preacher. His entry★ of Tuesday, June 9, 1772 relates, "preacht in the evening at Stonington point to a numerous and attentive audience;

★ Quotations are "as is" in the original text. Often, recording clerks took down names (and words) phonetically, as I do, too.

lodged with Mr. John Rathbun [sic]; he and Mr. Sands Niles appear to be sensable christians and maintain a meeting in that settlement (which is very considerable) only as they go to communion with Eldr Simeon Browns church."

Backus' journals tell us the first Stonington Long Point Baptist Church "was constituted down at the harbor April 22, 1775." A news entry of August 30, 1775, records that the Baptist church was built in Stonington Village at 161–3 Water Street and dedicated August 30, 1775, John Rathbone, First Pastor. (*Stonington Chronology* by Williams Haynes, p. 41.)

The historian George H. Minor obtained in 1894 some itinerant historical church records and related documents. He published the *Manual of the First Baptist Church.*, shedding light in this salient excerpt:

> There were present at the birth of this [Long Point Baptist] church some twenty or thirty delegates from the surrounding towns. No one knows positively who they were, nor is there any record of those who organized themselves into a church...That faithful band of Christians met here and there, now in private houses, now in the old school house, and in an upper hall near the corner of Grand and Water.
>
> Mr. John Rathbun was chosen their first pastor. He had been a leader among them or a lay-preacher and licentiate. *He lived here, built and occupied the dwelling house in which afterwards Dr. William Hyde, Senior, lived and died.* He served them four years then removed to the Baptist church in Ashford and was ordained March 15, 1781." [Emphasis added.]

The third pastor of the Baptist Church at Stonington Long Point was John Rathbone's son. Reverend Minor recorded that in 1784 "Valentine Wightman Rathbun, the son of the first minister" was called by the church to "ordination and pastorate." He remained for eleven years.

The Stonington Historical Society took possession in 1948 of four volumes of these Baptist Church records (1772-1916), and in 1992, John V. Hinshaw published transcripts of the first two volumes (1772-1848) with an illuminating preface and index listing more than a thousand names.

These newly published records are evidence that history about a small village community and its inhabitants need not be dull. It is a microcosm of human interrelation in the right proportion and scale. As Hinshaw concludes in his introduction:

> But it is also the raw data of our forbearers' lives. The characters and events may seem irrelevant today, but if you look back through history, you will see yourself reflected many times over, cast in different roles. These musty archives can be enlightening.

Remember, people in 18th-century New England tended to spend time together in religious meetings; these regular meetings were often the only social event. The agendas included, for the most part, more than God. Most likely in these regular convocations there grew a sense not only of community spirit and cooperation but also of seminal ideas about responsible democracy, liberty and union. The ambivalent 1775 colonial flag is half British Union Jack and half Liberty & Union on a brilliant red field. The incredible American success in the Revolution can be traced to more than a hundred years of village and town meetings in New England and along the colonies' east coast.

A central character in the earliest records of the Stonington Long Point Baptist Church is melancholy Sands Niles, the "sensable Christian" along with John Rathbone mentioned by Isaac Backus in his travel journals in 1772. Niles, a tireless, morally sensitive church clerk, recorded in his inimitable hand the minutes of what went on— ecclesiastically and otherwise. In 1782 he purchased the first transcribed church book and composed from his own precise recollection and the memories of others, the previous ten years, leaving three blank pages for the war years 1777–79.

Sands Niles was, if nothing else, a stickler for high morality. He made this startling entry on January 29, 1785: "Brother Rathbun [Valentine, John's son] proposed whether frolicking, such as fidling and dancing...was not inconsistent with the religion of Jesus?" The Stonington Long Point Church voted that it was. The stage was then set for Sands Niles' old Testament judgment and wrath.

Niles, one day, deeply concerned and aggrieved, was compelled to write down this passage:

> There are doubtless many nominal professors of Christianity that argue that fidling and dancing is an innocent recreation. But every christian under the present exercise of Grace knows it is not serving God, and if not serving him, it is serving the Devil...We are commanded to withdraw from every Brother that walketh disorderly.

No pusillanimous permissiveness here, 200 years ago.

Yet this was not the end of it. The final entry of church clerk

Sands Niles was on March 2, 1791. This time he recorded that he was again grieved by "carnal frolick, of fidling and dancing" by the daughter of Reverend John Rathbone. The minutes show Reverend Rathbone's promise to "restrain" his daughter. Niles was tentatively mollified and "concluded to endeavor to get along with the church, Etc." This heroic effort at tolerance didn't work, and soon after Niles sadly resigned as recording clerk of the church.

Niles died in 1799 at age 72 after a long illness and was buried in Robinson Cemetery in Stonington Village. It may have killed him to have suffered the severe grievance "at the conduct of Brother John Rathbun, for his not restraining his daughter from going and attending on a vain and carnal frolick of fidling and dancing, it being inconsistent and contrary to...the Gospel."

Well into 1848 the church minutes reflect prickly censure and discipline of varied church members for their perceived misbehavior, such as the "crime of fornification," "habitual use of Profane Language" and sometimes mere absence from church or Communion. The Baptists believed that members must live up to high standards of morality and habit, day to day, with no backsliding. The imbibing of alcoholic beverage was included.

In 1848, even prominent Dr. William Hyde, the village doctor, while living with his wife Rhoda Palmer at the Reverend John Rathbone house, was charged several times to come before the church meeting to answer, if the doctor could, for his "practice of letting [his leased-out houses] for the traffic of ardent spirits."

Dr. Hyde was outraged, refused to be summoned and on July 10, 1848, a letter he had written to the First Baptist Church in Stonington Village was read to the astonished congregation:

Beloved Brethren, [Dr. Hyde began]

It becomes my painful duty to address You on a Most important, interesting and solemn subject: being that of the low, barren and shattered condition of the Church, its Government, Discipline of its members &c, &c. which has been a great grief to Me and caused me many hours of solemn reflection for months past. Although repeatedly and strenuously have I laboured for Peace and harmony in the church on Gospel principles and my church covenant obligations but finding it like water spilt on dry ground under the disagreeable necessity of withdrawing my Fellowship and Membership from said Baptist Church disclaiming against all illegal proceedings, that I may not be a partaker in other men's sins.

That *Peace, Harmony, Brotherly Love* and genuine *Christian Charity* may again be restored to the said church is the *ardent* prayer of Your unworthy Servant.

Stonington, July 10th, 1848

William Hyde

The church members present then dutifully took up discussion of what to do about their distinguished member, Dr. Hyde. A resolution was offered to have the pastor "visit Dr. Hyde." The motion was lost, only three voting for it. "It was felt," the minutes reflected, "that the tone of the letter forbade any further labour." Then this abrupt resolution was presented and was passed, according to the minutes:

That the hand of fellowship be withdrawn from William Hyde & that he be excluded from this Church...

Dr. Hyde and his wife, hearing of his excommunication by the First Baptist Church of Stonington Village, thereupon joined the Village Second Congregational Church on Main Street. The doctor was a man of pride. Born in Stonington, he had graduated from Harvard Medical School, served as a state representative and was for many years president of the Stonington Bank chartered in 1822.

Upon his death on September 25, 1873, at 65, his devoted wife (christened Sarah Williams Palmer) gave him a large colorful memorial window that we noticed one Sunday while drifting away from an over-long sermon. Four years later when she herself died on May 18, 1877, next to the doctor's memorial window was erected her own memorial window—kindly, I'm sure, carefully, and paid for by her in advance.

7.

Origin of Reverend John Rathbone House in 1775

The Year of the First British Attack

I

As local historian Grace Denison Wheeler recorded in her local history of village houses:

> On the corner of Water and Harmony streets we see the long, low house [the gable roof came later] *known as the old Dr. Wm. Hyde place, built by Rev. John Rathbone, the first Baptist minister of the Stonington [Village or Long Point] Church in 1775.*
>
> Later he sold it to Dr. William Hyde who married [local belle] Rhoda Palmer in 1808, who lived and died here [in the Rathbone House].
>
> He was the good doctor for every household and was sent for, no matter who was sick and what was the cause for wanting him.
>
> The Doctor would come in with a good deal of bluster and fuss, and sometimes with some good-natured profanity, and before

he saw the patient or investigated the trouble, he would call Nancy Brown to go get the bowl and bandages necessary for blood letting, and then would follow the examination of the tongue and the operation of phlebotomy to the amount of a bowl full of fluid of which it is now considered so necessary to have a good supply if the invalid had consumptive tendencies.

This was considered a most important step, to get relieved of a surplus of bad blood from which the patient was suffering; this was followed by copious portions of calomel and julep and if the person had a good constitution, there was perhaps an even chance of recovery....

This [Rathbone-Hyde] house had been altered but little, and the small office on the south side so long used by the old Doctor and his son is still there [now the small Brown-Stoddard study].★

At the same time when Reverend John Rathbone was cajoling his church carpenter friends to build his house on highland facing south to the Point, the British chose to pressure their prime colony for tax revenues, ignoring decrees of self-representation granted to the colonists for decades. These pressures grew fiercely in 1774, leading to the first battle in April, 1775, in Lexington and Concord. Food for the British in surrounded Boston was short in the spring of 1775, when a foraging British frigate H.M.S. *Rose* attacked Stonington Village, threatening to bombard and destroy unless the village surrendered its food and cattle.

★ Excerpts: *Homes of Our Ancestors in Stonington, Connecticut* (1903), pp. 108-110, by Grace Denison Wheeler, daughter of Richard Anson Wheeler, author, *History of Stonington* (The Day Publishing Company, New London, Conn., 1900).

II
The Unheralded First British Attack
on Stonington Village
August 30, 1775

Most people know of the August, 1814, attack by the British on Stonington Village at the Point, when a squadron of naval invaders blasted away with cannon and fire to extort food during the enigmatic War of 1812. Yet few are aware of a startling attack by the British at the same Point of the village in 1775, 37 years earlier, when the stalwart villagers distinguished themselves with valor and stubborn ingenuity.

Stonington had already shown eloquent and active sympathy for the inhabitants of Boston in their resistance to Britain's arrogant usurpation of colony autonomy and demands for colony taxation without representation long before the Declaration of Independence on July 4, 1776.

Stonington's first historian, Richard Anson Wheeler, recounted the circumstances of the August, 1775, attack by the British on Stonington Village:

> Recall on Wednesday, April 19, 1775 the British soldiers battled the patriots at Lexington. The hinge swings here to war for independence. Connecticut was alerted to the "crisis alarm" and responded with vigor and spirit. Stonington elected a Committee of Correspondence and soon began "to furnish men and means to enable them to maintain their liberties." Stonington soldiers took part in the Battle of Bunker Hill in 1774 and thereafter in almost every battle of the Revolution.
>
> Cutting off British Supplies in Boston in 1774 and 1775

impelled the British to forage for supplies all along the coast of New England, and further west and south.

Crusty Commander James Wallace of the British Navy (44 years old and a 30 year veteran) was advised by local Tories "that Stonington was rich in the requisite food for an army and navy... brought here on a vessel and landed at Long Point..." Wallace sailed his 20 gun frigate H.M.S. Rose to Stonington Long Point on August 30, 1775, torrents of rain falling all day, and "sent a boat ashore with a preemptory demand for a delivery of said cattle to him, threatening terrible vengeance in case of noncompliance."

Receiving a flat Yankee refusal, Wallace sent his tender sloop up Stonington Harbor to bring off the cattle and any other supplies they could find. Resilient residents of Long Point were aroused to its defense.

Capt. William Stanton marched men in his command to the Point from near the [village] Green at Robinson's fields, joined by men under the command of Capt. Oliver Smith. Their Queen Anne muskets were effective if not decisive at long range.

At Brown's Wharf at the Point, the Stonington forces opened keen fire upon the enemy which caused their route with "severe loss."

For several hours Wallace's frigate H.M.S. Rose cannonaded Stonington Village. Wallace was surprised by the vigor of the defense and soon gave up any plan to land and burn the recalcitrant village. Wallace hovered about for a week and then disappeared for good.

Stonington Village was the only place in the colony during this anxious period that successfully resisted this British marauder. Norman Francis Boas tells us, "The attack on Stonington [Village] was the only naval attack on the shores of Connecticut during the Revolution and the first time that a British naval force was repulsed by the colonists." Told of the Stonington Village triumph, General George Washington, in Cambridge, saluted the "spirit and zeal" of this singular achievement. In September, the Connecticut General Assembly ordered enlistment of fifty men under (promoted) Major Oliver Smith for the defense of Stonington Village.*

Evidence of the first attack upon Stonington Village remained for many years: Traces of cannon shot through some of the houses were plainly visible when the village was attacked by British Captain Hardy in 1814. (Hardy was deputy to Lord Nelson during Napoleon's defeat at Trafalgar and was with Nelson on his flag ship when he died on the cabin sofa.)

The die was cast; the provoked American Revolution for Liberty and Union was about to commence. The British king had been unreasonable or indifferent and so had the muddling Parliament, prodding its most valuable colony, grown independent and prosperous, to rebel and finally declare its total independence in 1776.

* See *Stonington During the American Revolution,* by Norman Francis Boas (Seaport Autographs, Mystic, Conn. 1990).

8.

Stonington Family Diaries Provide Rare Legacy of Colonial Life and Times Covering Almost a Century

Let us turn for a moment to a broader canvass of colonial life and times before the commencement of the American Revolution in relation to Stonington Village.

Thomas Minor, a lion of a man, kept an unusual diary of his activities around Stonington and about his active leadership in important events from 1653 (or 1654) until July of 1684. His son, Manasseh, also a virile leader, continued the practice of the diary into the 18th century. Manesseh's diary—even more brief and cryptic—covers the period 1696 to 1720. For this seminal colonial period of the early New England colonists, these illuminating daily records are two of only 18 known to exist.

Descendant John A. Miner wrote in 1976, when both historic diaries were reprinted:

A land and a culture were carved out of a wilderness at a cost far beyond our understanding. Perhaps by looking back through the actual days, months and years in the lives of these early pioneers, we can regain a sense of proportion for our own lives.

The two diaries give valuable insights into how a village begins, organizes and survives in a wild land of wolves, bears, rattlesnakes and hostile Indians.

Thomas Minor had not, as the first diary says, come to New England with John Winthrop on "the good ship Arbella." In fact he arrived in Salem, Massachusetts in July, 1629, as a passenger on the ship, *Lyon's Whelps*. After ten years in this pleasant neighborhood he came down to Stonington (then called Southernton) to stay awhile at Wequetequock Cove, north and upstream from the Stonington Village peninsula.

Finally, after a land deed mix-up, Thomas Minor decided to settle permanently in Quiambaug (a neck of land east of Mason's Island to the west of Stonington Village and still the homestead of the Minor family—now spelled Miner) on property he acquired by grant of the General Court for his services to the colony with the Indians. It is here in Stonington that he built his house overlooking Fishers Island Sound and began his diary, which he continued for thirty years.

In the 1899 edition of *The Diary of Thomas Minor* the editors' introduction provides the significance and essence of the Thomas Minor family's lives and activities, not just a postcard or faded photograph found in an old attic:

> In the life of Thomas Minor we have a prominent example of those men, who with their families, came to this country and fulfilled the purpose of time in creating in the new world a people of illimitable resources, jealous of personal rights, with brawny arms and fertile brain and with unconquerable perseverance so characteristic of the

pioneer settler who attacked the forces of nature's wilderness that a nation might be built for the world to respect.

Thomas Minor married Grace Palmer, daughter of Walter Palmer, a founder of Stonington. He helped organize the first church (First Congregational, north of the Stonington Village, called the Old Road Church—still going strong) and served it well. On April 24, 1669, he wrote a succinct résumé in his diary:

> I Thomas Minor am... sixty-one years ould. I was by the Towne and this yeare chosen to be a selectman the Townes Treasurer, the Townes Recorder, the brander of horses, by the General Courte Recorded the head officer of the Traine band, by the same Courte of the ffour that have the charge of the milishia of the whole Countie, and chossen and sworn Commissioner and one to assist in keeping the Countie Courte.

Suddenly, in 1675—a hundred years before Reverend John Rathbone persuaded church carpenters to raise his house on Water Street—the most severe Indian uprising of the colonial period occurred. Despite being 68 years of age, Thomas Minor joined all the men of the village and environs to take an active part in the great Swamp Fight near Kingston, Rhode Island, on December 19. His sons were with him in this crucial bloody ordeal. There were horrendous preparations, training, deployment of militia and negotiations with friendly and hostile Indians in anticipation of the terrible life-and-death confrontation and in the vain hope that the awful conflict could be avoided.

Thomas Minor's diary records: "From the 8 of december [1675] to the 8 of ffebrarie [1676] I was Imployed in the Countrie service about the Indian Warr besides 8 days in the sumer hors and man and my white horse Ten days being prest for [Captain] John Gallop [a hero of Stonington who was slain in this Swamp Fight]."

In the battle there was bitter suffering and a great number of casualties on both sides. The misery continued on the following day as the surviving colonists and their Indian allies struggled to return home through a deep snowfall.

The Indian War had begun when certain Indian tribes became determined to wipe out all the colonists. There had been forty years of relative peace since the vindictive struggles with the Pequots that culminated in the Mystic victory. All New England, from Maine to southeast Connecticut, was riveted with terror at the news that the colonists were again subject to extermination.

Their worst fears were realized when the Indian grand chief, King Philip, led a savage and determined horde of warriors across New England. The opposition was led by Simon Willard. The threat to the colonists and their families was unnerving. The flow of new colonists to the Connecticut River valley congealed.

Connecticut, Rhode Island and Massachusetts were especially vulnerable to the assault. The Mohegans were powerful and undecisive; they had been induced by King Philip intermittently to attack colonists' homes and settlements. The loyalty of Uncas, chief of the Mohegans, was uncertain; the dread increased.

On June 24, 1675—five months before the decisive Swamp Fight—King Philip struck a heavy blow, burning houses and slaughtering men in Rhode Island. Governor Winthrop, who was ill, was petitioned frantically for assistance. After wavering, the Mohegans, together with the Pequots and Nahantics, joined the colonists. This fortunate alliance made the survival of the English on this New World soil possible.

The heat of the battle centered within Massachussetts and in the villages along the Connecticut River, but as winter approached, the hostile Indians concentrated their forces in the Narragansett territory, dangerously near the Connecticut frontier and Stonington.

The whole colony, in effect, went under martial law. New London, Norwich and Stonington were fortified. Church belfries became lookouts and signal points. An army of a thousand men was raised. Connecticut troops were under the command of Major Robert Treat, of Milford; New London under Captain John Mason; Pequots and Mohegans under Captain John Gallop of Stonington.

Provisions of pork, beef, corn, rum, horses and carts were laboriously obtained, and the army desperately marched in conjunction with troops from neighboring colonies to engage the Indian enemy in Rhode Island on December 19, 1675.

At great sacrifice on both sides, a victory was obtained in the Swamp Fight. More than a thousand Indians were killed. Among the Colonists, 200 were killed and wounded, eighty of whom were of the Connecticut line. The Swamp Fight ended the Indian War. The troops finally returned to Connecticut in August and were ordered by the General Council to disband and go home. The leader of the Uprising, King Philip, was finally pursued and slain on August 12, 1676, by soldiers from the Plymouth plantation. There was extensive follow up the next year ordered by the Colonists' new ally, the Mohegan leader, Uncas.

The catastrophic war with the Indians was over—the second battle of extermination was at an end. The colonists and new settlers could now, at last, look to the future, and the flow of newcomers commenced once again.

PART TWO

I

Experience shows that a very populous city can
seldom, if ever, be properly governed; all
well-governed cities have a limited population.

ARISTOTLE,
POLITICS

II

Cities are the abyss of the human species. At the
end of a few generations in them races perish or degenerate,
and it is necessary to renew them. This renewal always comes
from the country.

JEAN-JACQUES ROUSSEAU,
ÉMILE

III

Man is now only more active—not more happy—not more
wise, than he was six thousand years ago.

EDGAR ALLAN POE

IV

"Do any human beings ever realize life while they live it?—
every, every minute?" asks Emily, in Thorton Wilder's *Our
Town*. (Now a ghost, Emily laments the joys of a daily life that
once seemed humdrum.)

V

We possess of our past only what we love,—and we want to
possess everything we've lived through.

RAINER MARIA RILKE

9.

George Washington Whistler and the Stonington Railroad-Steamboat Enterprise

Stonington history includes the unusual story of Connecticut's first passenger railroad—a significant and valiant time in the development of the village.

On November 10, 1837 the first railroad station in the state of Connecticut was built on Main Street. An able West Point graduate engineer Major George Washington Whistler, created the Stonington Railroad. It ran from the Village Dock on the harbor in Stonington Village to Pawcatuck, Connecticut, on the border of Rhode Island—a historical feat (although less than five miles long) because it was the first Connecticut passenger railroad.

Major George Washington Whistler brought his wife and children to Stonington Village. He was the able father of master painter James Abbott McNeill Whistler, who made an indelible if flamboyant mark on world art and is known for wit and devotion to exquisite qualities of light and color.

As I write this account at the eastern end of the second floor of
the Rathbone house, I can see out the window to a red house that
has a white plaque. It says that, while Major Whistler was in Saint
Petersburg drawing the plans for an important railroad line to
Moscow for Czar Nicholas I, his wife and children, one of whom
was James Whistler, lived in the house.

To my right, on the corner of Main and Wall streets, with a red-
lacquered Japanese tea ceremony garden, is the handsome cream and
putty clapboard house built by Captain Amos Palmer in 1787. The
plaque on that house says that for a period while Major Whistler was
in Russia, guiding the czar's railroad development, the mother and
her children lived there for a time also. It belonged to Dr. Charles E.
Palmer, a benefactor-mentor who followed Major Whistler to
Russia. This is the same fine house in which many years later lived
the 20th-century author Stephen Vincent Bénet and his wife,
Rosemary.

Between these two dwellings, one on Harmony Street and the
other on Wall Street, and directly behind our cottage, is the large
white Nicholas Palmer mansion, now home to the Holy Ghost
Society.

In addition to the Stonington Railroad, Major George Whistler
developed through his ingenuity the first railroad extension to link
New York and Boston. The key to this success, before bridges and
tracks along the Connecticut shore, was colorful steamboats that
sailed overnight through Long Island Sound between New York and
Stonington Village. At the Village Dock terminus, passengers and
freight were loaded and unloaded. A rail line was constructed from a

spot adjacent to the Second Congregational Church on Main Street to Providence. There a ferry crossing the river to India Point connected with the Boston to Providence line. The fare for passengers six cents a mile.

On November 10, 1837, the Stonington-Providence Railroad opened with a grand celebration. (A week later the village restricted railroad speed in the borough to five miles per hour.) The railroad built the large Hotel Wadawanuck on the Common, now the site of the Stonington Free Library. The Hotel Wadawanuck was a center of summer visitation and intrigue, food and drink, for years. Except for those who cannot pronounce its name, its memories of social joy linger on.

Stonington Village historian Tod Johnstone, a railroad buff, displays an amazing model railroad of Stonington Village's Dock (as of 1883) at his Anguilla Gallery, 72 Water Street, in the village. He says that Whistler's rail link from New York to Boston was successful because this travel option was so superior and a far less perilous trip than rounding Point Judith, Rhode Island, the Cape Hatteras of the North, on a boat. Making the safe connection, he says, earned the Stonington Railroad the "prestigious nickname of 'Old Reliable.'"

(Major George Washington Whistler died in Russia in 1849 and was buried at Calvary Episcopal Church in Stonington Village)

In 1889 the Thames River was bridged, completing the New York to Boston overland service and—sadly—eliminating the need for (and the romance of) a steamboat connection. By the year 1904 the excitement and the glory of the Stonington Railroad was over.

Today up Main Street toward Elm, all that is left of this enterprise is a bronze plaque on a stone rock on the front lawn of the Second Congregational Church, which is now called the United Church. It commemorates the location of Major George Washington Whistler's first railroad station in Connecticut.

10.

Vistas of Village Architecture, Seascapes and Secret Gardens

It is during this brief span of existence in time that
I must live the timeless, that is: eternity.

FREDERICK FRANK

Stonington Village can be savored on foot. This is the best way to observe the roads, lanes and magical byways, at different times of day and different seasons. This village is not a seasonal resort; it is beautiful and resourceful the year around. Snow in winter is magical. In this latitude, changes of the season are clear-cut and welcome.

The extent of unhurried exploration is mercifully small, and the eye picks up penetrating vistas and detail at each point in the walk—pictures of sea and sky, soaring oaks and maples, white yielding beech, blossoming apple and lilac, mountain laurel, purple-pink hydrangea and honest rhododendron—and then surprising glimpses of small secret gardens, that are revealed more openly in all their glory every few summers by the ladies of the Village Garden Club.

Along the way one begins to know the houses as friends. The "Report of the Historic District Study Committee Borough of

Stonington (1991)," lends intelligence to what you see. The committee has tried, unsuccessfully so far, to persuade a two-thirds majority of the borough property owners to protect an area of historic value from architectural alteration that would be visible from the street *unless* approved by the borough commission. Despite this study showing that the time has come for the village to adopt such an ordinance to "protect the character of the village," the necessary votes have not been obtained.

The reason may be that village property owners come from (or have absorbed) a long New England tradition, fashioned in small villages, of fierce independence and self-reliance. Many villagers simply do not want, at this juncture, to be told by government what they can and cannot do with their own property. Characteristically, they point out, with a shrug, that Stonington Village has come a long way for 350 years in beauty and picturesque harmony without the constraint of an arbitrary ordinance.

Out of the ashes of defeat of the historic district proposal did remain the phoenix of the village study, a veritable audit of the villager's inheritance.

Here are several examples of what the walker can find, in a short time, in Stonington Village today:

- *Colonel Oliver Smith house,* 25 Main Street, c. 1761. Gambrel roof, sturdy colonial center chimney. One of the oldest and most quintessential houses in the village. Oliver Smith was the major in charge of the militia that first repelled the British invaders in August, 1775, at Stonington Point.
- *Captain Edmund Fanning house,* 44 Main Street, c. 1760. He was first to sail around the world under the flag of the United States; a classic house, restored.

- *Gilbert Fanning house,* 38 Main Street, c. 1760. Was once run by Gilbert Fanning as a tavern.
- *Thomas Ash house,* 5 Main Street, c. 1780. Thomas Ash was a rope maker. His delightfully restored cottage was moved from the Colonel Joseph Smith house site. Now part of the Gurdon Trumbull Estate.
- *Aunt Mary Howe house,* 52 Main Street, c. 1814. Small scale, gambrel roofed, simple charming detail. Once rented as the village library.
- *Jonathan Waldron house,* 39 Water Street, c. 1783. Sustained bomb damage during the British squadron attack of August, 1814.
- *Nathaniel Eels house,* 49 Main Street, c. 1785. Simple Georgian elegance.
- *Lodowick Niles house,* 68 Main Street, c. 1797. Greek Revival front entry. Georgian stairway. Handsome cast- iron fence. Marvelous flower, fruit, and vegetable garden.
- *Colonel Joseph Smith house,* 51 Main Street, c. 1800. Federal style, double-hipped roof, pedimented entrance with leaded fan light, central bay.
- *Captain Amos Palmer house,* 24 Main Street, c.1787. Imposing ship's captain house with raised basement and Japanese tea ceremony garden. As noted, the artist James Abbott McNeill Whistler lived here as a child with his mother; so did the distinguished poet Stephen Vincent Benét and his wife, Rosemary, in the mid-20th century.
- *Reverend Hezekiah Woodruff house,* c. 1789. Federal house with widow's walk, terraced gardens.
- *Peleg Hancox house,* 33 Main Street, c. 1820. Handsome authoritative Greek Revival. Temple-front with four fluted ionic

columns, simple lunette in the pediment. Awninged porch overlooking colorful garden.

- *Charles P. Williams house,* 37 Main Street, c. 1825. Greek Revival, temple facade, ionic columns. C. P. Williams, an owner of whaling ships, moved the house from site of Ocean Bank on Cannon Square.
- *The Ocean Bank, Cannon Square,* c. 1851. Greek Revival. In 1990, while being stripped for painting, the original gold lettering "OCEAN BANK" was discovered and has been retained. Now owned by the Stonington Historical Society.
- *The Custom house,* 16 Main Street, c. 1822. Built to house the Stonington Bank, chartered in 1822. Dr. William Hyde was president for many years. Stonington Custom District was established in 1842.
- *The Arcade,* 61 Water Street, c. 1830. Greek Revival commercial building with doric colonnade. Has been whaling office, fish market, bakery, drug store, jewelry store—now attractive apartments.
- *The United Church, formerly the Second Congregational Church,* Main and Elm streets, c. 1834. Handsome Greek Revival building, four huge doric columns and square two-story clock (black-faced) tower, visible to the whole village, which tells us the time and has struck the hours since 1838—more than 150 years of bonging and still going strong. Memorial windows for Dr. William Hyde and his wife, who bought the Reverend John Rathbone house and lived there for their lifetimes. Recent Pastor Steven Burt is also a poet and an innovative teacher.
- *Peleg Hancox House,* 168 Water Street, c. 1848. Majestically dominates Wadawanuck Square, singing the wealth and zest of whaling days. Greek Revival frieze; symmetrical tall chimney.

Cream white and secure. (An 1820 Peleg Hancox house is on Main Street.)

- *Gurdon Trumbull house,* 7 Main Street, c. 1840. Federal form with Greek Revival decoration; recessed entrance with two handsome fluted ionic columns. Lantern on roof recalls the village's seafaring past. Dominates Cannon Square, looking out to sea; on the east side, lawn vistas, flower gardens and trees down to Little Narraganset Bay.

- *Stonington Lighthouse,* Stonington Point, c. 1842. Gothic Revival. Earlier lighthouse nearer the tip of the Point was being undermined. Stone by stone rebuilt on high ground a few yards to the north. Discontinued as lighthouse in 1926. Purchased by the Stonington Historical Society for $3,650; has been the society's museum since 1927. At the top see fascinating panoramas of village, sea, sailing and motor vessels, islands, sounds and ocean. Louise Pettiway, curator.

- *Gurden Pendleton house,* 2 Cannon Square, c. 1848. Stately Federal form with applied detail in Tuscan or Italianate style. Attractive white picket fence.

- *John F. Trumbull house,* 85 Main Street, c. 1860. The mansion presiding over Wadawanuck Square is done in French Second Empire style and has its own internal park.

- *The Stonington Free Library,* Wadawanuck Square, c. 1899. Renaissance Revival designed by New York architects Clinton and Russell. Compatible addition 1990. Well proportioned, on site of 19th-century Wadawanuck Hotel of steamboat days. Lots of grass and large trees provide welcome breathing space. Around this Common Stonington Village takes out all the stops and celebrates with gusto its annual Village Fair in August. No one misses this.

- *Calvary Episcopal Church,* Church Street, c. 1847. Gothic Revival. Designed by noted architect Richard Upjohn, reflecting Saint James the Less in Philadelphia (1846-49), which follows the form of Saint Michael's, Long Stanton, Cambridgeshire (c. 1230). Upjohn, a high churchman, was the architect of Trinity Church, at the foot of Wall Street, New York City. Over the protests of the vestry, Upjohn installed a large cross on the steeple; the vestry left it intact only because of the cost of its removal. The current rector of Calvary, Reverend Mark K. J. Robinson, introduced to village life his wife, Eleanor, and three young daughters, Sewell, Frances and Florence.

11.

Curious Note on the Artist James Abbott McNeill Whistler

James Abbott McNeill Whistler, painter, etcher, wit and eccentric, was born in Lowell, Massachusetts. He suffered early on being dismissed from West Point for insufficient knowledge of chemistry. In 1855 he went to Paris, where he acquired a life-long appreciation for the works of Velazquez and for oriental art, particularly Japanese prints.

Regarding his painting "Falling Rocket: Nocturne in Black and Gold," Whistler sued art critic John Ruskin in 1878 in London for writing that Whistler asked "two hundred guineas for flinging a pot of paint on the public's face." In court, Whistler defended his work by saying that the harmonious arrangement of light, form and color was the most significant element of his paintings. To de-emphasize their subjective content, he testified, he entitled them, by fanciful, abstract names such as "Arrangement in Gray and Black"—the famed portrait of his mother for example, in the Louvre.

At one point in the famous trial the pompous counsel for John Ruskin asked Whistler, with keen British sarcasm, on cross-examination: "Just tell the jury how many hours you *actually* spent on this painting for which you ask a fortune?" Pausing just a moment,

Whistler shot back: "A lifetime." The jury exploded. Whistler won the verdict in court, but payment of the court costs left him bankrupt.

Whistler's celebrated lecture "The Gentle Art of Making Enemies" (1890) was a witty collection of clips from his critics with his own biting rejoinders.

I've always suspected that Whistler picked up his superb genius of light, form and color from his early days in Stonington Village.

12.

Cardinals Are
Village Lovers

There are unexpected events that may occur in Stonington Village that give us wonder and often a smile.

One early summer morning in the strong east light striking off Little Naragansett Bay, I felt a flutter of red across our small Zen garden. Looking out the window, I saw, for the first time, a resplendent red cardinal, in full regalia, and then, busy in another part of the enclosure, a female mate, beige for security, and evidently intent on finding and creating a nest, perhaps in this little space. I was fascinated: Had we been blessed by the arrival of a pair of cardinals?

What happened next amazed me. We had arranged with an ingenious mason-contractor, Mark Pascatello, to encase the high wooden walls around the yard with a crisscross trellis over applied mirrors. Alexandra one day had discovered such a trellis-mirror detail in a trim French garden in Fontainebleau. The resulting effect for light, expansion of space and reflection is magical. The small garden grows better, and the sun sparkles and dances on the surface of the mirrors.

The two cardinals had found in our garden a serendipitous use for housing and games. The female cardinal dove down with a flutter of unerring precision from the tall lilac tree into and through the small diamond-shaped opening between the wooden trellis slats to a four-inch board platform. Once inside and alighted, she pecked with vigor and excitement at her image in the mirror. The male cardinal observed the process like a foreman from his sedentary perch on the lilac tree.

Here, the cardinals surely speculated, was the perfect nesting home, *au naturale,* free from the predation of cats and squirrels. Here was an abode with illusory (mirrored) feathered friends of the same endearing species.

After five days of this diving in and out, the beloved pair of nesting cardinals inexplicably disappeared from the garden, and their inimitable "tweet-tweet-tweet" was heard no more. Alexandra and I felt a deep sadness that we had lost two friends.

Nine months later, just after the commencement of spring in 1995, we again had a sweet surprise in the dappling sun of the morning. First the sounds of "tweet-tweet-tweet." Then, we spotted the male cardinal, resplendent in his red robe, looking proud and a bit plumper, bouncing on a branch of the lilac tree. We peeked from an upstairs window. Then Alexandra pointed. *There,* within the trellis, on a platform, pecking fondly at the mirror, was the red cardinal's mate, back home after almost a year away—happy as a bird.

13.
Quimper Faïence
A Village Link
With Brittany

Stonington Village has an attractive shop on Water Street, at number 141, that imports and sells the world-renowned colorful pottery, each piece signed "HB/Henriot Quimper."

The coincidence of the Stonington Quimper Faïence story has a timeless ring that serves to highlight and bless the spirit of this enduring Village.

A Stonington Village couple, Sarah and Paul Jannsen, found their house at the foot of Wall Street overlooking Little Narraganset Bay. This spot in earlier days was once the site of the local pottery maker. The Jannsens recognized the striking similarity of the village's landscape, seascape and maritime activities with that of the village of Quimper, an ancient cathedral town in southwestern Brittany at the juncture of the Steir and Odets rivers. (The Breton word *kemper* means "confluence.")

The Jannsens opened a shop in the village to import tableware from Faïenceries de Quimper, a large factory on the Route de Bénodet that had produced handmade pieces of artistic quality for 300 years. But the old factory came on difficult days and slipped into liquidation in the summer of 1983. The Jannsens bought the property, thus preserving the continuity of faïence art: distinctive pieces such as charming plates, pitchers, cups handpainted with traditional peasant figures, roosters and flowers.

The old method of painting by hand has been maintained. At the 1690 faïencerie site—the incomparable *coup de pinceau,* the stroke of the brush. The Stonington Village Jannsen corporation on Water Street now directs internationally the manufacture and the wholesale and retail sales of Quimper Faïence. This resurrected artistic activity adds pleasure and color to Stonington Village.

14.
Villages Hit by Hurricanes
East Hampton, Mystic, Watch Hill and Stonington Village

Like love, village life is not always smooth and placid. Because Stonington Village juts out toward Block Island Sound and the Atlantic Ocean, the records have revealed, since the earliest days, the cruel effects of hurricanes. It is discomforting that the word "hurricane" comes from the West Indian "huracán," or "evil spirit," and perhaps that is why hurricanes were called "gales" until the twentieth century.

The first recorded gales to strike Stonington, Watch Hill and Mystic occurred in the early days of the 17th century, according to Thomas Minor's diary: "a greate storme of wind and high tides—pieces of vessel cast ashore…; much loss of corn and hay; many trees blown down."

As late as 1750 there were no houses on the peninsula called Stonington Point. Until then, the land that is now Stonington Village (or Borough) was used solely for grazing and for drying fishing nets.

After 1750 the village grew swiftly and by 1775, as we have seen, had more than 500 inhabitants. Main Street was laid out on August 10, 1752, and was soon blessed with towering elm trees. Sadly, in later years they were destroyed by a wicked combination of hurricanes and Dutch elm disease.

On September 23-24, 1815, the Great Hurricane hit Stonington Village. Many ships were driven ashore and many houses destroyed along the coast. Much land washed away from the sides of the Point, where the house of Captain Benjamin Morrill with his child and a relative inside was swept out to sea in their home and drowned. Widow Anna Loper's house was also totally destroyed, but she was saved—carried to shore by Richard, her 16-year old-son. The hurrican left debris 15 feet deep on Water Street.

For 123 years no ocean fury devastated the Stonington coastline—so naturally the inhabitants and municipal officials slumbered. No realistic plans were made to meet a similar challenge in another era. Houses and cottages were built along the water's edge at places where prescient Indians would have been more cautious.

In the summer of 1938 my parents rented, from Decoration Day until after Labor Day, the Minor house on the Atlantic coast beach at the end of Lily Pond Lane in the idyllic village of East Hampton, Long Island, New York. This summer is remembered by four children as a sunny, carefree time in our lives.

East Hampton was then a small attractive home-sweet-home village that had been laid out lovingly in the 17th century, and was centered around family, farming and fishing. In the 1930s, it was our summer place for swimming in herculean blue-green ocean surf; walking on wide, isolated sandy beaches; having hearty picnics on the dunes; bicycling along winding tar roads; playing vigorous tennis at Maidstone (supervised by little Ernie Clark); and dancing and playing amateur golf at the handsome main Maidstone clubhouse high above the ocean to the west. It was a heavenly environment. Self-appointed arbiters say that around this time was the apex of perfect summer for East Hampton as a village.

What we loved the most in those days—just before the advancing storms of World War II—were the dawn ocean swims directly from the beach in front of the house. There were no lifeguards, so my mother, head out her bedroom window, would worry as her four impulsive teenage children headed with glee into an enormous pounding surf. The waves built twelve or fifteen feet and crashed down on the tender body surfers under a few feet of water—unless we caught the waves, arms and legs stretched out, and soared into shore sixty yards or more until we were beached on the wet sand, with the ocean retreating to the origin surf to do the entire classic rhythm all over again.

My father worked until noon on Saturday at the Stock Exchange in downtown Wall Street and did not arrive on the Long Island Rail Road "Cannonball," tired and hot, until late afternoon. Meeting him at the East Hampton Village station was a command performance for my mother and the four children. Jack Bouvier, known as Black Jack to the elders, the father of Jacqueline Kennedy Onassis and a classmate of my father at Yale, also would be on the Cannonball, but he always looked more tailored and cool as the express train took him to the preceding Southampton, a spiffier watering hole at the time, where he would charm everyone over a Saturday night dry martini.

———

It was ingrained in my father to see to it that the Minor summer cottage on the dunes was "picked up"—that the stretch of beach in front of the house be cleared of all detritus and debris. Neat as a pin, he would say.

One day my brother George and I, coming out exhausted from the surf, noticed a large wooden crate being noisily buffeted by strong waves eastward along the beach in front of the house. We knew this eyesore of a box would be an irritant to our father upon his arrival on Saturday, so we set about the engineering feat of pushing and hauling to make it move with the tide on down the beach. It ended up in front of the Louis Connicks' summer house.

When we picked up father at the station that Saturday, he had some interesting news for us, heard on the radio, about what an unusual thing had happened on the beach in East Hampton Village. A large crate of Special Reserve Dewars White Label Scotch (his favorite) had washed up—out of the blue—on the Connicks' beach, to the delight of harried New York corporate lawyer Louis Connick. My father inquired earnestly of George and me, "Isn't that an *interesting* stroke of good fortune?" There was a long silence. I looked at George. He looked down. And I said, innocently, "Yes, that is a very interesting coincidence..."

By Labor Day the surf at the Minor cottage had become more turbulent,—"dangerous" said my mother, who was, in fairness, one of the best surf riders in the village at that time. The autumn storms were definitely upon us; we knew the summer was waning and we would soon have to return, reluctantly, to boarding school in Middletown, Delaware.

That September, a summer resident of East Hampton stopped by Abercrombie and Fitch on Madison Avenue in New York City to purchase a mahogany barometer for his beach house. When he took it to East Hampton he became terribly upset because the instrument was defective: it failed to register properly the serenity of the Indian summer days in the village. Angrily, he returned his barometer to Abercrombie and Fitch and made an exasperated complaint.

While the John Wanamaker customer in those days was always right, this East Hampton summer resident was startled to find upon returning to East Hampton that the sky was black and the Atlantic Ocean surf was up, even ballistic. The radio came on strong, apocalyptic, reporting with alarm that residents were facing a disastrous hurricane, whose arrow of destruction was aimed at the eastern end of Long Island (East Hampton) and the eastern end of the southern New England shore (Mystic, Stonington Village and Watch Hill).

Ever cautious, our family got in the station wagon with our school clothes and tennis racquets, locked the doors of the Minor house, precarious on high dunes above a snarling, heaving ocean surf, and left for New York City. I do not know what happened to the man who huffily returned his barometer. I do know that a lawyer of the same name as mine (with whom I was later sometimes confused), Peter Campbell Brown, learned with deep sadness at his New York City law office, that his wife and several children, while in their summer house nearby on the beach of Westhampton Village, had been swept out to sea.

Stonington Village was hit at the same time by the massive September, 1938, hurricane—viciously, with a force equivalent to mountains of exploding brick, with rushing waves of an angry ocean sweeping, whipping, driving, disrupting, smashing, flooding. Sailboats—all boats—popped out of their water habitats and landed adjacent to houses, buildings and the shoreline railroad.

Water, under huge atmospheric pressure and storm, has no limit in its mass destruction. Man and nature yield. People tell us it will not happen again. But it will.

On Wednesday, September 21, the 1938 hurricane smashed Stonington Village, Mystic and Watch Hill with the destruction of a blitzkrieg. No fury like it had been recorded since 1815. Wind velocities rose to 186 miles per hour. A Watch Hill church, Christ Episcopal, held its annual picnic for ladies that fateful day at nearby Napatree Beach. A tidal wave swept out to sea and drowned 10 women in the group. All 44 cottages on Napatree Beach were destroyed and washed away. Eastern Wall Street in Stonington Village, just south of our cottage in Stonington, had many small houses that were carried away by this ferocious hurricane in one afternoon.

In its course the 1938 hurricane killed 488 people; 1,754 people were injured, 8,924 summer cottages and homes were reduced to rubble or oblivion. More than 6,000 boats were wrecked. The 1938 hurricane caused more damage than any other tropical storm recorded in the world.

I was with Alexandra in the Stonington Village cottage in 1992 when the radio told us, in spades, that the next day we would suffer

"Hurricane Bob" (now all hurricanes are named, for some reason). On cue, the sky darkened, the storms raged, the sea rose up and covered the harbor docks. We were in for it. The radio reports grew more gloomy. The 1938 debacle was recalled ominously once, then again and again. We were upstairs getting ready to fly the next day from Providence to Toronto.

Suddenly, down Water Street, drenched in flashing rain, came the village's red Neptune fire engine, simonized and world class. Its speaker blared out, "Take notice! All residents! Evacuate! Go now! Hurricane Bob is a danger to all residents of this coast, particularly Stonington Village."

We were stunned and bewildered. What could we do? We had no car. The weather was blackening and horrible. A decision had to be made. We looked out the second-story window and remembered the dramatic David McCullough television documentary about the horrors inflicted on Watch Hill, Rhode Island and Stonington Village by the 1938 hurricane.

Our cottage was built on a high rise of land, away from the harbor, with one of the first solid stone-lined basements, a stand-up, dry, under-room.

The Hurricane Bob alarm grew more hysterical. We talked more about what we should do; time was running out. Looking into Alexandra's wondering eyes as she watched the neighbor Elliotts' dock virtually disappear in rushing rising water, I asked her what she felt we should do, as the fire truck circled Water Street to deliver once again its urgent message to evacuate.

Alexandra replied, "What do *you* think?" I said, "Well, this house is 217 years old and has always been here on this foundation, through years of gales and hurricanes. *We're staying!*" Alexandra agreed And we stayed while Hurricane Bob roared and beat on the house, and then swerved to do its severest damage to Watch Hill and the villages along the southern Rhode Island shore. We flew out gratefully the next morning.

15.

Village Summer Resorts Becoming Year Round
Mantoloking and Bay Head

More than a century ago, sensible visionaries chose to create small villages adjacent to the Atlantic Ocean beach front, each several miles, on the beautiful central shore of New Jersey. Mantoloking and Bay Head gained early notice as respectable, if exclusive, family village summer resorts—a new phenomena at the time across America.

Both Mantoloking and Bay Head are about two and a half miles long, straddling slim barrier islands between roaring ocean and vibrant, diamond-studded Barnegat Bay. Bay Head has more off-beach land for shops and parking. Smaller at the waist, Mantoloking has rarely had shops and contents its development to a post office, yacht club, tennis courts and sailing-boat basin. One main road and one railroad line slice through the narrow outer bank. Developed in the early 20th century, the railroad at first brought families from Philadelphia to settle both villages. Later, the line connected with Newark and New York.

The comfortable, shingled family cottages that were built in the late 19th century became the ultimate places to enjoy traditional, close-knit family summers, swimming in the celebrated Atlantic Ocean surf and walking the slight brick and board walks, fully dressed, parasol in hand. Sunburn was anathma and nudity shunned. And within a thousand yards of the ocean were the unforgettable glories afforded by Barnegat Bay—sailing, boating, fishing, and canoeing up rivers and streams. The Bay afforded families of these two neighboring villages unparalleled sailboat activities and eager competitions that produced, over a hundred years, some of the best amateur sailors in the world.

Here is a treasured environment—dedicated unashamedly to summer and to healthy outdoor activities. The heady atmosphere implanted memories that remained for years, lodged indelibly in the villagers as fervent nostalgia.

I first visited Bay Head, I'm told, when three or four years old, coming up with family from main line Philadelphia for summer visits, probably with relatives at a cottage on the beach.

My infantile recollection is sufficiently blurred to be of little significance except for the strong primal smells of salt air, ozone and burning wood, and for mental pictures of close, large-size cottages surrounded by generous porches supplied with white wicker furniture and of gentle sandy roads, jubilant flags flying (indicating—*in residence*) and the endless miles of broad beaches where I was introduced to the treat of picnics on the dunes. My mother had been given these pleasures in her own young summers away from townhouse Philadelphia, on the same ocean, and wanted me to experience them too.

———

Recently, friends from New York invited Alexandra and me to come down one winter weekend to their seaside cottage in Mantoloking. Alexandra had spent several years designing the renovation of the cottage to the fine taste and requirements of the owners, who, following the new pattern, drove down regularly from New York, both summer and winter. I'd heard a great deal about this beach house, but until this visit I had not seen it restored and embellished in its grand indigenous style; as Alexandra would say, "simplicity, appropriateness and beauty." I was not disappointed. The house is a joy.

From this pleasant experience, I learned that 5,000 people now live the year around in Bay Head; in summer the population overflows into myriad cottages, houses and small inns. Mantoloking remains smaller, slimmer and perhaps prouder with 390 cottages, many of which are enjoyed the year around. The good shops of Bay Head are utilized with great success.

No place can be fully appreciated without some bit of knowledge about its origins, triumphs and travails.

In the fall of 1609, the logbook of Henry Hudson's *Half Moon* presents the first recorded glimpse of the entrancing Barnegat Bay region. The exploring ship nosed up the inlet to the south until, the logbook reflects, coming within sight of a "great lake of water [Barnegat Bay] being drowned land which made it rise like islands, which was in length ten leagues. The mouth of the lake [the inlet] had many shoals, and the sea breaks upon them as it is cast out of the mouth of it...And we had a great stream out of the bay...Far to the north of us we saw high hills [New Jersey highlands]...This is a very good land to fall in with and a pleasant land to see."

Customs die hard. In the late 19th century residents of these two resort village communities performed a summer bathing ritual that had been introduced by the local Lenni-Lenape tribe of Indians. The great event was variously called Salt Water Day, Great Wash Day, Big Sea Day or Beach Feast Day. Thousands of people came from miles around—the mainland, localities adjoining Monmouth, Burlington and Ocean counties, on an annual basis. They frolicked in the surf, engaged in a country fair atmosphere replete with amusements, vendors of all kinds and lively sideshows; bathed in the sun and, most memorably, gorged on corn and baked clams. Pits would be dug in the sand and fired by burning kindling; the clams would be leveled across the heated fire, and then covered with layers of seaweed. The result was a culinary treat the revelers and gourmands would not forget.

The clambake tradition is hardly unique to the New Jersey shore. I have experienced this outdoor marine delight for many years along the East Coast: at Quogue, East Hampton, Bridgehampton, Bay Shore, Babylon's barrier islands (e.g. Fire Island) and Montauk, all on Long Island; and also at Martha's Vineyard, Nantucket, Cape Cod and the coast and islands of Maine. A Monhegan Island clambake of July, 1948, is still imprinted.

So exuberant did some of these celebrations of summer and the beach become that, early in the 20th century, Wreck Pond near the village of Sea Girt, to the north of Bay Head, sternly prohibited the clambake ritual on the grounds that the participants, in the opinion of the police marshal had behaved like Roman pagans. He declared primly that the revelers had become "too decidedly unconventional." You might say they were carried away.

There always seems to be some good soul who will tell the story of a beloved community. One who wrote with poignant reflection about Mantoloking was Frederic R. Colie in *An Exercise in Nostalgia—Mantoloking 1880-1920* (Compton Press, 1970).

In 1875, Frederick Downer, assisted by New York lawyer Frank L. Hall, dared to assemble land between Bay Head and the south border of Mantoloking. The landscape then was a wiry mesh of sumac, bayberry, cat brier and, yes, poison ivy. To reach this incipient development the visitor had to travel by sail or rowboat. Soon the emerging resort was named Mantoloking, which means "Land of Sunrise" in the Lenni-Lenapi Indian tongue. The sunset is likewise also magnificent across Barnegat Bay.

A decade later the village resort began to stand up and walk. The public was invited to buy lots fronting the ocean—100 x 250 feet or 100 x 150, between Ocean Avenue and the ocean. The prices ran between $500 and $3,000. "Terms easy," lured the sales agent, Seashore Improvement Company of Mantoloking, in 1883. "The place is advancing rapidly. Now is the time to purchase," an advertisement predicted in the *Courier,* a local paper in Toms River. A rebate of 10 percent was allowed for those who built within a year from the date of purchase. Nothing is new.

By 1909, before you could say Henry Ford, there appeared to be an automobile traffic problem on the narrow barrier island. The Mantoloking Village Committee was petitioned to limit car speed to ten miles an hour.

We would be unaware of the subtle but memorable beauty of this Mantoloking village resort in the 19th century were it not for a weekly publication called *The Snipe*, which printed a column by a talented watercolorist named Miss Lisa Downer. In addition to painting the environs of central Mantoloking, Miss Downer, in her column in *The Snipe,* made word pictures about the beautiful flora underfoot.

Few know what rare and beautiful flowers bloom here; the weird beach rose clings ghostlike in the sand, pale yellow primroses make great patches of grass gay with their opening and closing petals and nowhere are pink and white marsh mallows more stately.

The wild roses vie with those of Mount Desert in redness and sweetness; the dainty beach pea with its tiny blossom, bud and curling tendril, its whole existence within the limit of a few inches; magnificent purple and white iris waving their flags of France; the butterfly weed spreads its long trails of fiery color, the scarlet lobelias or cardinal flower makes a brave show when August bids it come.

Lisa Downer continued her enthusiastic vein—more poetry than prose—based on her own keen observation:

Great purple spikes of king flowers loom up, their feet in watery places; golden rod, beautiful, bewitching, has its home in great variety and richness. It is so tall and heavy with bloom as it dances and waves in the salt breezes, giving life and color to the whole beach, asters, daisies and laughing black-eyed susans come early and late.

Loveliest of all…are the centaurs or sentries. They carpet great stretches of meadow with their pinkness, overcoming with bloom the meadows soft green of the gentian family and fairy like in elegance they wave and toss in every shade and scale of pink…

Orchids love this boundless wealth of air…moccasins or ladyslipper is the most abundant. Heavy grassy plumes nod everywhere, purple gorse, star-eyed grasses cover acres and in the sweet white cones of alder are concealed many a tiny spring of sweet water which filters through the sand...

By now out of breath, Downer ironically concluded:

Many people come and many people go who see nothing but sand and grass.

In 1911 Mantoloking became an incorporated borough as did Bay Head and other neighboring villages in New Jersey, following the self-rule principle of ancient British boroughs. Mantoloking was then obliged to elect a mayor, six councilmen, a tax collector and an assessor. But there was a problem: There were not enough citizens in the new borough to fill out both the Republican and Democratic petitions, as required by law. Nevertheless, no one contested the election, and the new borough was born.

On the winter day when we arrived at the beach cottage of our friends in Mantoloking, the sky was somberly overcast and the surf was wild with rough criss-crossing waves. Over 120 years, the sea had crept closer and closer to the cottages just above the dunes.

Despite the gray inclement weather, three black–rubber–suited surfboarders were darting through the huge waves toward a vantage point farther out to sea. At the appropriate moment, each chose to ride a mammoth curling wave, with graceful skill, smoothly in to the shore: each of them then secured his surfboard and gingerly went out to sea and did the trick all over again.

The next day, Sunday, was different. The storms had receded. The mysterious ocean had calmed down, was more orderly in advancing its waves toward the beach. The flat winter sun shone white midday light on the glaring surface of the sea. Who was that, I wondered, observing three similar black figures bobbing out over the waves. I was looking out from the bedroom window seat on the second floor of the cottage. What were they doing? Then I realized that these swimmers were not surfers but three fat happy ducks that were perfectly content, in deep winter, not to fly south but to stay in Mantoloking, a century-old village community founded for families who love the simple pleasures of life on the natural ocean beach.

16.
Farming Village
Middletown, Delaware

In the Great Depression years of 1935–40, I lived as a boarding high school student close to a farming village called Middletown 25 miles south of Wilmington, Delaware.

In the center of Middletown's cluster of turn-of-the-century houses and elms was the village square with its memorial to World War I veterans, the unhurried Middletown Hotel, a pharmacy selling everything, a dry goods shop;, a newspaper store with girlie magazines in the back, Mr. Jones' two-chair barber shop with outside red-striped pole, ex-wrestler Plato Momopopulis' Hamburg Restaurant known more colloquially as "The Greek's", a hardware and feed store, an ice cream parlor that sold long red Pall Mall cigarettes ("For Discriminating Taste"); and the old movie theater, grinding out double features with popcorn on Saturday night.

Two miles or so south of the village was Saint Andrew's School, founded in 1931 by Felix du Pont with a handful of boys, an outstanding faculty, memorable school nurse Meg Miller who watched our health with eagle eye, ordained headmaster Walden Pell II, deputy headmaster John MacInnes (coach of the 1939 undefeated "Boilermakers" football team): Bill Cameron, John Ellis Large, called Don, and several other stars. The small campus in fieldstone gothic overlooked serene Noxingtown Pond, which was long enough for competitive crew in four and eight shiny shellacked amber shells. Ball-playing turf had been cut from cornfields. The Cochran family farm was within view of the school, surrounded by acres of asparagus (an unappreciated staple served at every meal except breakfast). Its defining silo rose against expansive sky. We could smell its odoriferous horse and cow barns and squealing pigs, fed amply from the school garbage in V-shaped troughs.

Saint Andrew's, a half century later, is not the same sea of bustling construction and make-do for a community of boys and teachers struggling, against odds, to instill "character" and "self-reliance." The battle then was not always successful. Many of us, I now know, were not at our best. There may be something about farming village quietness that serves to ignite delinquency and adolescent revolt.

Saint Andrew's was the site of the 1989 movie *Dead Poets Society,* which displays to the delight of Middletown's early graduates a handsome array of field-stone buildings, arching colonades, spires, dormatories, a boat dock, gyms, a swimming pool and, crowning it all, a varied forest of great trees where there were virtually none before. They were planted for 25 years, with vision and perseverance, by far-sighted Walden Pell II, a noble man. Blessed is he who plants trees under the shade of which he will never sit.

As I remember, our small satellite school was never isolated from the village of nearby Middletown. We wandered on foot across the flat, bucolic landscape of fences and cornfields and around the verdant shores of Silver Lake. Sometimes, as a privilege, we rode in the rumble seat of school housekeeper Miss Machalis' open coupe, which we secretly called "The Flying Coffin"; at other times we slugged along in the old gray school bus operated by apple-cheeked superintendent Steve Foley. Everybody made the rounds to town, where the excitement of parole and soda pop were always to be found. Although fed enormous amounts of food three times a day, we were always hungry, as I recall. Teenage starvation.

Mr. Jones, the genial white-haired village barber, sometimes came to school to cut hair, armed with his menacing electric comb, endlessly clicking scissors and a lethal straight razor with a leather strap (reminding us of earlier disciplines at home). Momopopulis, the wrestler turned restaurateur, came annually in black professional suit and tie around his size 18 collar to lecture us on the intricate maneuvers of the Peloponnesian Wars. He related the tale of the young Spartan student who harbored his pet fox under his shirt and would not disturb the decorum of class by crying out when the fox began eating into his stomach. The talks linger with us today and sometimes enter our dreams.

Sunday was occasion to take the "ungrounded" students into Middletown for church services at red-bricked Old Saint Anne's, rife with pre-Revolutionary history (Delaware was the first to join the Union), and to a larger, less historic church where, as I recall, the itchy, twitchy student body was more difficult to control. Faculty masters sat in the back pews recording the breaches of discipline, such as a "hot foot" or slug to the ear of a boy in front. I do not remember the sermons, but one hymn still rings in my ears—"Jesus calls us, o'er the tumult." It was the fashion to be irreverent; it takes time to grow up.

The Depression of the 1930s was deeply felt in the agricultural villages of Delaware. Family farms could not make ends meet and were painfully foreclosed. Banks failed and life savings were gone. Franklin Roosevelt and his brain trust declared a New Deal, with fanfare, but its programs' benefits trickled down slowly upon the

Middletown farming community. Yet, if not more chickens in the pot and a new tractor, we felt there was a growing seed of hope.

In 1936, to the dismay of Headmaster Pell, I campaigned fruitlessly, as a ninth grader, for Alf Landon for President—the Sunflower candidate from Kansas. Landon took winning electoral votes only in Vermont and Maine. Roosevelt won the school vote and the country with a landslide. Delaware went Democrat, and the farmers around the village generously invited us to a victory barbecue of a whole cow and a spirited torchlit night in Middletown village.

17.
Lyme Villages, Fenwick and Old Saybrook
Almost a New Empire

Bordered by the eastern side of the magnificent Connecticut River and Long Island Sound, some of the most tranquil villages can be found. For the most part they are ancient and sing of pre-Revolutionary history and a tradition—even now—of living intelligently and well.

Several favorites I've appreciated for more than half a century are Old Lyme, Lyme, Fenwick and Old Saybrook. They are picturesque jewels strung along the shoreline railroad. There is access to memorable small sea-beaches and sailing and motorboating on the broad river that Adrian Block scouted in his nosy sloop *Restless* before the Pilgrims landed.

Harper's Magazine published an article about this sublime area in 1876 (republished in 1976 by the Old Lyme Bicentennial Commission). It revealed with its 19th century time frame and focus some odd facts and surprising stories that most of us have forgotten, or never knew.

The anonymous author of the *Harper's* article walked from the tiny train station toward the village of Lyme:

> From Noyes Hill…you obtain your first glimpse of the village, or rather of its roots and chimneys and spires among the treetops; also of Meetinghouse Hill beyond, of the salt meadows and Long Island Sound to the right, and of the beautiful river, formerly the harbor for merchant vessels whcn Lyme was a shipping port, winding lazily to the sea in the foreground. The ferry road crosses a snug New England bridge, and guides you to the Pierrepont House, a new summer hotel…just outside the wealth of shade which shields the town.

The hotel was named after an early minister of Lyme, a brother of the wife of Reverend Jonathan Edwards, who in 1722 was drowned while crossing the Connecticut River on his return from a visit "to his lady-love" in New Haven. Sweet demise.

Lyme was settled in 1666 and for 350 years has boasted a perfect climate for health, intellectual creativity and longevity. Who could ask for more? The New York City *Harper's* author was surely taken wholeheartedly with this benevolent region as he piously proclaimed the virtues of its location and residents:

Lyme was "near enough [to] the metropolis to partake of its literary culture and many-sided opportunities, and sufficiently remote to escape its dissipating wastes, and it has always maintained a self-respecting inner life..."

Then, even more effusively: "Lyme is, or ought to be famous for its lawyers, as it has produced more than any other town of its size on this continent, or any other…and not only lawyers 'whose trade it is to question every thing, yield nothing and talk by the hour: but eminent judges, senators and governors, its latest and grandest achievement being a Chief Justice of the United States [Morrison R. Waite]."

We are led by the masked author to the village along "The Street," described as easy old-fashioned elegance, a mile and a half long, "wide enough to swallow a whole family of New York City streets, lined with handsome grandfatherly-looking trees, and mansions, some modest, some pretentious, some antique,...planted on either side of it at neighborly distances. Your eye will fall upon two churches [the spires!], an academy, a post office, two or three stores, where groceries, hardware, and dry-goods dwell in harmony together, a milliner's shop with peaches and melons and shoe horses. Signs of business there are none. The scene is one of tranquillity on a broad scale."

When passing the illustrious Waite family mansion, the author said that an ancestor Waite was, in the time of Oliver Cromwell, a member of Parliament and one of the judges who precariously signed the death warrant of King Charles I. After the Restoration of the monarchy, we are told, the English Waites, fearing retribution, fled to the New World, settling first in Sudbury, Massachusetts, in 1677 (where Reverend Edmund Brown, the first proprietor of this village, was probably having a hard time with its younger generation).

Noyes Hill is then described as the site of homes of a notable pioneer family. The first minister of Lyme was Reverend Moses Noyes,★ who preached for a record 63 years. What endurance on the part of the congregation! He was one of the first graduates of

★ Descendant of the Noyes so disappointed with the insurrection in Sudbury in the mid-17th century.

Harvard and one of the founders of Yale. It was his brother James Noyes who was the first minister of the First Congregational Church in Stonington, the Old Road Church on Agreement Hill.

Lyme used to be a part of Old Saybrook, which was settled in 1635. Oliver Cromwell personally selected Saybrook as the ideal place for the commencement of a New World empire, dissatisfied as he and the Roundheads were with the royal rule of civil and religious affairs under to-be-beheaded Charles I. John Winthrop, the younger, was dispatched to build a fort on a slim peninsula at the mouth of the Connecticut River. It was called Saybrook, in honor of Lord Say and Lord Brook, both of whom headed the New Empire Enterprise but neither of whom ever did arrive in their namesake village and fort.

Two large squares were laid out on the verdant plain surrounding the fort, anticipating the building here, with panoramic views of the sea, of great houses for the wealthy and the powerful—refugees from royal tyranny and fantasizing leaders of the mystical dream of the New Empire.

The only English leader who did appear at the Saybrook fort and common was Colonel George Fenwick. He came to live here with his "young, lovely, golden-haired, sunny-tempered wife, Lady Alice Boteler," who, we are assured, made the "quaint fort bright with wild flowers and merry with laughter."

Poor Cromwell, embarking for Saybrook from the Thames in London, was stopped abruptly by an order, *Non Exit,* from the King and never accomplished his wistful mission of empire in Old Saybrook. Soon after, Colonel Fenwick, saddened by the untimely death of his beloved Lady Alice, returned to England, where he was one of the judges who tried and condemned to death beleaguered Charles I.

Saybrook, some may recall, was the seat of the first Yale College. The books in its initial library were donated by Congregational ministers, including James Noyes, the first minister in Stonington. This Yale campus enjoyed fifteen commencements until the magnetic forces of New Haven took Yale away, despite the avid objection of citizens of Lyme and Saybrook.

In the summer of 1718, the governor of Connecticut and his royal council descended on Saybrook with a royal warrant for the sheriff to convey the precious college library to New Haven. Using force against strong local resistance, the sheriff finally seized the books and put them under guard for the night. In the morning every wagon for transportation of the books was found broken, and the horses had disappeared into the countryside. The persistent sheriff obtained other carts and horses, but then he found that the adamant advocates of Saybrook and Lyme as Yales' proper location had destroyed all the bridges on the road to New Haven. When he did finally get through with the carts after great frustration and delay, he discovered more chicanery: more than 300 books were missing, as well as valuable documents, manuscripts and papers. Who knows when these will turn up for the precious archives of the Bienecke Library?

That 1876 *Harper's* article provides a picture of Old Saybrook— "five miles or more of sea-beach, presided over by Fenwick Hall, a great elegant summer hotel, which draws annually hundreds of visitors..."

Today, Fenwick on the seashore is one of Connecticut's eight boroughs (like Stonington Village) and has been preserved as an attractive summer colony village. Katharine Hepburn has a summer home on the Fenwick shore. I saw her energetically playing tennis and looking much like Lady Alice, one balmy day, as I drove around by the sea in a spare golf cart.

18.

The Influence of the Village on René Dubos

In 1972, the sensitive scientist and author, René Dubos, published his second book, *A God Within* (Charles Scribner), an illuminating exploration and psychological analysis of who we are and where, properly oriented, we have the potential of going in a turbulent world. Like Emerson, he was always searching for ways and means to find *how* and *where* we should live.

Alexandra and I thought Dr. Dubos' book was stimulating and rewarding. We decided to seek him out for more edification and inspiration. Through the energetic Dean James Morton of the Cathedral of Saint John the Divine and his wife, Pam, we were introduced to Dr. René Dubos and his wife, Jean, at the deanery after the dean and Dubos had delivered a pungent dialogue sermon.

Conversations with Dr. Dubos led to further meetings when we tried to absorb his genius in understanding why we are all here; his message about size, scale, smaller numbers and the value of the village as the place to live; and how we should, on our own, develop a deeper insight into our own possibilities to contribute to life on this earth.

As our friendship and admiration for Dr. Dubos grew, I began to wonder how his own mind and spirit had developed. How had he come to conceive the attitudes and outlook he expressed with searching precision and truth in his books? They grew to more than thirty in his lifetime—and won him praise, fame and a Pulitzer Prize. On his deathbed at Saint Luke's Hospital, he was composing another chapter of another book, Jean by his side.

René Dubos in person, in lecture and in his books was always clear and concise. His illustrations were instantly helpful to understanding. Without patronizing, Dubos gathered an uplifted following and perhaps caused a strengthening of optimistic viewpoints in critical areas throughout the world. This wise person made a difference in our society.

We learned that René Dubos grew up in a "very small village...outside the mainstream of the modern world" despite being only thirty miles north of Paris. The name of the village, Hénonville, is not on the map. Ironically, Hénonville today, and vast areas surrounding, is now the Charles de Gaulle Airport, the major airport for Paris. Dubos never once left Hénonville until he was a teenager. What kind of experience did he receive in a small village without the touted stimuli of Paris, an hour or two by bicycle to the south? Maybe the best. He said:

> Limited as village life was, it provided a rich variety of experiences which are still alive in my memory and which are indeed incarnated in my whole organic being. As is probably the case for all children, I was bewitched not only by the persons and places I actually knew but perhaps just as much by the persons and places I imagined during hours of daydreaming. This enchantment...has conditioned my whole life...

My early remembrances are therefore of a world which I could directly see, hear, smell, and touch. There was the one-room school house which also served as *city* hall for the 450 inhabitants; a thirteenth-century church with lichen-covered walls in the center of the village; farms with numerous domestic animals; hills *so accessible* that the highest of them was the site of the cemetery; small woodlands here and there; muddy ponds crowded with frogs, eel and carp; immense fields of wheat, alfalfa, and sugar beets, separated by narrow country roads leading on to other small villages a few miles away.

Dubos spoke to us often about what it is that we ultimately want from life. About where to choose to live (if you can) in order to live fully. He understood the give and take of any choice. We must decide and then courageously accept consequences.

Our perceptions would sharpen when he would say, as he often did, that we human beings are not substantially different in biological response from persons in the Stone Age:

Modern man is still psychologically conditioned by the range of human contacts that were possible during the Stone Age. He commonly finds village life stultifying and boring, *yet he needs it emotionally.* He spends much of his leisure time traveling in search of village atmosphere and he endlessly illustrates it in novels and paintings.

As early as the 1970s, Dubos recognized that we moderns try to recreate the village within the urban agglomeration with block parties and demands for self-management of districts, neighborhoods and boroughs.

Dubos reminded us that, even though cities have existed for

many thousands of years, most people during prehistory and the greater part of history have lived in groups of "relatively small size—whether as nomadic tribes or as village dwellers." He cited Peter Laslett's study "The World We Have Lost" to show that villages of some 500 inhabitants constituted the fundamental demographic unit of England until the Industrial Revolution.

Summarizing his *The God Within,* Dubos startlingly concluded that whether a man or woman is part of a hunting tribe, an industrial city, or a late-20th century corporation, both seem to function best in groups of fewer than a thousand persons and find it difficult and perhaps awkward personally to deal with many more than a dozen. "From time immemorial," Dubos observed, "armies have been organized on a similar numerical basis." Twelve soldiers in the scouting party; twelve disciples for the religious leader. Organizations invariably decline as they expand. Smallness is good, said David; Goliath giants fall down.

While always a reputable scientist, meticulous in his research and judgment, René Dubos was also ever the poet and the optimist. He looked upon a tumultuous and dangerous world. As he gently assured us, he had lived through many springs. He could still smell the rich farm soil of his native village and the colored crayons and chalk in the one-room schoolhouse. He believed to the end of his life that, while it may be difficult to retain faith in the destiny of mankind, it would be cowardice to despair in the light of our past journey and experience.

Few, I believe, have so eloquently taught the essential importance of the small community and the genius and spirit of the village.

19.

Villages of Northwestern Connecticut

To find a thread of villages and explore them all on a day trip is a wonderful privilege. An example can be found in northwestern Connecticut. This region is still largely unspoiled by intruding city folks, and its pristine villages show in many ways the independent spirit and character of earlier days in America.

Time does not allow in this book fair treatment of these exceptional places where, from all accounts, people are living well in a setting of simplicity, appropriateness and beauty.

But as you travel north on Route 7, the following eight villages are on your right along the picturesque Housatonic River, where Kent crews in springtime dream of Henley.

- Cornwall Bridge
- Cornwall Village
- North Cornwall
- West Cornwall
- Falls River
- Canaan
- (Touring Around and South) Salisbury
- Lakeville

These communities in the northwest corner of Connecticut have characteristics in common with other villages in New England yet each has an imprint of its own, a uniqueness that is a precious quality and spirit of place. A tour or brief visit may not reveal the particular essence that endears the village to its inhabitants. But I think we may say that time lived in any of these communities can be a fulfilling experience, because of their human scale, simple yet handsome architecture and sense of history.

It is, of course, in part the relative isolation from metropolitan mega-cities that lends the air of purity, fresh zest and simplicity to these villages. Here we may find certain newly recognized feelings that are, as discussed, biologically satisfying.

Some people, we recognize, are disoriented by village life—whether in New England, Ohio or southern France. What attracts some people to the village distracts others.

Living in different urban, suburban and village communities for almost three-quarters of a century has taught me that there are trade-offs for each place that must be weighed. We know there is no perfect location. Even in Heaven a person may grow tired of playing the harp.

"Most people spend their entire lives believing that happiness is just around the corner," says Timothy Miller, a teaching clinical psychologist, "yet our natural desire for just a 'little more'—more prosperity, more love, more success or power seems to have no 'off' switch."

We take our feelings and attitudes with us wherever we choose to live. Dr. Miller believes that wanting more, demanding more, can be a fundamental obstacle to spiritual and emotional development. He reminds us that teachers of wisdom throughout the ages have taught that the secret of true happiness is to *want what you have*.

PART THREE

I

To him whose elastic and vigorous thought keeps pace with
the sun, the day is a perpetual morning.

HENRY DAVID THOREAU,
WALDEN

II

Before green apples blush,

Before green nuts embrown,

Why, one day in the country

Is worth a month in town.

—CHRISTINA ROSSETTI (1830-1894),
SUMMER

III

If it's out of scale, it doesn't work.

—ABBY ALDRICH ROCKEFELLER
quoted by her son David Rockefeller

IV

We never value life enough when we have it.

—JACQUELINE KENNEDY
(writing to Richard Nixon after
President Kennedy's assassination.

20.

The Village of Concord

Concord, Massachusetts, viewed over a sweep of 360 years is unique. This village's history, on all its levels, is extraordinary. Its religion impacted the whole culture of New England. The seeds of responsible democracy and independence were planted here. And as for military ingenuity—prowess, village independence and bravery—the Revolution *started* here and in neighboring Lexington, with the "shot heard around the world." Literature blossomed in Concord a century later with Ralph Waldo Emerson, Louisa May Alcott, Nathaniel Hawthorne and Henry David Thoreau—the "blazing stars" of American Literature.

Here in Concord arose a culture of such quality and strength that *its* echo is still heard around the world.

On September 2, 1635, the General Court, sitting in Cambridge, granted Simon Willard, the Reverend Peter Buckeley, and several others:

A plantation att Musketaquid; there shall be 6 myles of land square to belong to it.

Peter Buckeley had arrived at Boston in 1635, a graduate of Saint John's College at Cambridge and already a strong and scholarly church leader. He had inherited from his father the rectorship of the Parish of Odell in Bedfordshire, England. For religious reasons, he chose to emigrate to New England and to gather a new congregation in Concord (now known as First Parish Church). William Stoughton in Boston said, "God sifted a whole nation [England] that he might send choice grain over into this wilderness."

Governor John Winthrop wrote in his journal that there were only about twelve families in all in the original emigration to Concord. He sent a crew of carpenters and lumber to build village buildings and the church meeting house. Early records indicate that Simon Willard was the leading layman. He and Peter Buckeley had arranged the purchase of the Concord land from the Indians. The settlement was to be located at the confluence of two rivers, as was Odell in England. A writer once described the visual similarities— "the same green meadows, the same upland plains, the same tranquil stream, meet the gaze in the one case as in the other."

It was a brave move away from civilization for the first inland settlement in New England. In the early years Concord was isolated and on its own. The separation may have induced reflection and serious conversation among dedicated settlers leading to the sacrificial glories to come.

The Concord village community and the church were in effect one unit until 1834, when the village slowly became a distinct and self-governing entity. This unity probably accounted for the exceptional influence on government policy of the clergy and the vestry of the First Parish Church for the first 200 years.

All of New England at this time, not just Concord, was close-knit and inbred. Virtually everyone was related. Propinquity is a great matchmaker. The same observation can be made about Stonington Village.

There have been only eighteen ministers of the First Parish Church in Concord since the beginning; the first was Peter Buckeley, the founding leader and refugee from Anglican intolerance. The fourth minister was an ancestor of mine, Joseph Estabrook.

In 1660 Joseph Estabrook had come to New England with his brother, Thomas. They sought, as Puritans, a greater freedom to practice their religion. Both enrolled in the Class of 1664 at Harvard College, a class which, I suspect, numbered no more than 25 students. The main course of study was religion.

In 1667, three years out of Harvard, Joseph Estabrook was ordained by the Reverend Edward Buckeley, who had succeeded his father at the Church. Estabrook became a colleague of Edward Buckeley's, and on Edward's death in 1696, he was selected to be the senior minister. He continued in this office until his death on September 16, 1711, at age 71.

Joseph Estabrook's son, Benjamin Estabrook, became the first minister in Lexington (then called Cambridge Farms) in 1696—79 years before that shot was heard around the world.

Of the death of Joseph Estabrook, the *Boston News Letter* of September 18, 1711, reported: "This day was interred in Concord the Reverend Joseph Estabrook, minister in said town for about forty years. He was eminent for his skill in the Hebrew language, and was a most orthodox, learned and worthy divine; of excellent principles in religion, indefatigable laborious in the ministry, and holy life and conversation."

The First Parish history reveals something of the thinking during Estabrook's ministry. At a morning service Reverend Estabrook once used a plate that happened to have the "hated" papal insignia on it.

An old deacon at the service, noticing the offensive cross and three nails of the crucifixion, threw the plate across the chancel, smashing it. Estabrook's son recovered the pieces and glued the plate together. This mended plate is now on exhibit in the Concord Antiquarian Museum. The meticulous parish history explains, "If feelings ran high, it was because the colonists had given up a great deal in coming to this strange land to found their Calvinist church, and were convinced that they were right."

While living in Concord, Estabrook was repeatedly urged to leave and go to Boston. They said "he was too bright a star to be muffled up in the woods amongst the savage Indians, and ought to come to Boston where he could do more good." He, however, thought differently and determined to stay in Concord among his "Indians." His salary at the church was eighty pounds a year, of which forty pounds was paid in money and the balance in grain and cuts of wood. We do not know that Joseph Estabrook ever complained.

Simon Willard, as a Puritan, had come to Massachusetts early in April, 1634, for religious freedom. He settled in the village of Cambridge and took up 100 acres with a house on it on the Brighton side of the Charles River. A merchant, he traded extensively with the Indians with whom, it was said, he maintained the best relations. He was a close friend of Peter Buckeley—both were strong men of eloquence and power.

Simon Willard, also an ancestor, according to the research of my grandfather John Adams Smith Brown, participated in Reverend Buckeley's services in Concord for years, was elected to the General Court and was appointed a judge for a period of thirty years. In addition, he was named chief military officer in the country, a position of responsibility in days when there was always the fear that one's sleep might be invaded by the sound of an Indian war whoop and the unnerving blow of a tomahawk—or worse, the shrieks of wife and children.

Subsequently, Willard sold his property in Concord and bought a farm at Still River, which is now Harvard College. After vigorous leadership in King Philip's Indian War, which brought devastation to Massachusetts and Connecticut, he died of influenza in 1676. Later members of the Simon Willard family became known for crafting reliable clocks. One ticktocks today in a reception room of the White House Oval Office.

The 18th century in Concord bore the increasing fruits of its highly qualified villagers. William Emerson, who was related to the Buckeley family, became the seventh minister of the First Parish Church ten years before the start of the Revolution. He was the distinguished grandfather of Ralph Waldo Emerson, the great essayist and thinker.

William Emerson was neither a Jonathan Edwards hell-fire evangelist nor a Unitarian or transcendentalist like some of his descendants. Rather, he applied somewhat pragmatic Christian principles to his daily life. These uncomplicated beliefs and actions interested him the most during a brave and forthright career.

William Emerson married Phoebe Bliss, daughter of the preceding minister, and was called as pastor in 1765. The village parish voted him a settlement of 200 pounds and an annual salary of 100 pounds. He built for Phoebe a house that became known as the Old Manse, on the bank of the Concord River by the Old North Bridge, overlooking what would become the most noteworthy Revolutionary War battlefield. William Emerson and Phoebe as well as the children were at their Old Manse home when the Redcoats came up the road from Lexington April 19, 1775. Nathaniel Hawthorne later lived here with his bride and, in his literature, made the Old Manse a warm, endearing village house in romantic literature. Here grandson Ralph Waldo Emerson came at 31 to write his first major work.

In October, 1774—with hostilities heating up dangerously—the provincial government of Massachusetts moved from Salem to Concord Village, where it voted its independence of the British Crown. William Emerson was its chaplain and John Hancock of Boston its president when the battle of the Old North Bridge took place in April, 1775. Emerson, despite his collar, was in the thick of it. The minutemen were his parishioners.

Emerson became a confidant of George Washington and was instrumental in guiding Harvard College to Concord Village when the Cambridge campus was occupied by the Continental troops in the autumn of 1775 and winter of 1775–76. Lectures were held in the church meetinghouse and the Village Town House. President Samuel Langdon of Harvard preached for Emerson often during this period.

In August, 1776, Emerson went as chaplain into the Continental Army. At Ticonderoga he was sadly discharged by General Gates for illness, a "billious fever" (which his grandson in his journal later called "camp fever"). He died suddenly on October 20 in Rutland, Vermont on the way home to Old Manse, never having returned to Phoebe and the children in Concord Village.

The next minister in Concord was Ezra Ripley, who, for a 50-year period, served as the only minister in the community. He eventually married Phoebe, his predecessor's widow, and gave to his church and neighborhood village a long and determined leadership. When

Ralph Waldo Emerson went to live for a while at the Old Manse after the death of his wife, Ellen, he found that his step-grandfather had taken over the entire heritage of his own grandfather, including his wife, his estate and his parish. An early biographer said archly that Pastor Ripley was "born to govern" and "was not a little arbitrary in the exercise of his sole authority as bishop of the place."

21.

Covenant
Reverend Peter Buckeley 1646

The first minister at Concord, Reverend Peter Buckeley, wrote and preached a great deal on his conception of man's Covenant with God. He wrote a strong book (published in London) *The Gospel Covenant; or The Covenant of Grace Opened,* which elucidated the debate at that time: —whether to find salvation (1) in a covenant entered into with God by good *works* "left to himselfe to stand by his own strength," or (2) by a covenant with a God of grace, where-by "God undertakes for us, to keep us through *faith.*"

Buckeley believed and preached the second conception of grace for salvation; salvation was possible only by commitment and faith in God's way and plan. Man was not permitted to wander liberally, committed only to "works" rather than "faith," as he saw it. This division of theological thought, imperfectly expressed here, formed a bedrock of controversy in Concord and the rest of New England. Remnants of the controversy remain to the present day.

John Winthrop, Puritan and governor, was Peter Buckeley's friend and co-leader in the Massachusetts Bay Colony. Winthrop on arrival in the New World wrote and spoke of his belief that New England would become "as a City set upon the Hill"—the ancient sacred city fixation. In 1646, when Buckeley wrote down the Covenant he espoused, he ended his proclamation on a theme of continuity:

> We (in New England) are as a City set upon a Hill, in the open view of all the earth. The eyes of the world are upon us, because we professe ourselves to be a people in Covenant with God.

When William Emerson was pastor of the Concord's First Parish Church less than a hundred years later, the lively debates about the nature of the covenant persisted. Ralph Waldo Emerson's grandfather wrote his own version of the covenant on July 11, 1776; he ended his proclamation this way, seemingly to tolerate slightly some compromise between strict faith and flexible works:

> And wherein our conduct as a church or particular members has been inconsistent with our solemn Vow, we renounce it humbly.
>   Now, sensible to some degree of the great Deceitfulness of our own Hearts, we desire to make constant application to the Throne of Grace for strength to keep this holy Covenant.

By the middle of the 20th century the First Parish Church had gone through intellectual and theological turmoil. It became Unitarian in the early 19th century, choosing to live its own life more by good works than solely by faith. It became quite independent, free to make its own adaptions to changing modes of religious thought and practice. Surely the shift in free thought, away from creed and covenant, would have been a surprise, if not an alarm, to those earlier fathers of Concord, Peter Buckeley, Edward Buckeley and Joseph Estabrook, as well as to John Winthrop and, certainly, John Calvin. In

1956 Reverend Edward Daniels (the fifteenth minister) made the change more concrete by proclaiming a new covenant for the First Church:

> It furnishes sanctuary to those who sincerely desire a refuge from the heat and tumult of the day. And at the same time it seeks to stimulate an active and intelligent response to the needs of the modern world and the demands of the modern spirit.

Three months before William Emerson proclaimed the covenant of his Concord parish, Paul Revere was alerting the countryside that the Redcoats—and the Revolution—were coming.

22.

The Crucial Year 1775
Paul Revere's Ride

For Americans, the year 1775 was most crucial. The following letter of a daring patriot and artist—Paul Revere—about his historic ride, April 18-19, 1775, may epitomize the taut tenor of the time. He penned this letter to a friend, Reverend Jeremy Belknap:

Dear Sir:

I set off upon a very good Horse; it was then about 11 o'Clock, & very pleasant. After I had passed Charlestown Neck, I saw two men on Horse back, under a Tree. When I got near them, I discovered they were British officers.

One tryed to git a head of me, & the other to take me. I turned my Horse very quick, & Galloped towards Charlestown neck, and then pushed for the Medford Road. The one who chased me, endeavoring to cut me off, got into a clay pond, near where the new Tavern is now built. I got clear of him, and went through Medford, over the Bridge, & up to Menotomy...

I found Messrs. Hancock & Adams at the Rev. Mr. Clark's; I told them my errand, & inquired for Mr. Daws; they said he had not been there; I related the story of the two officers, & supposed that He must have been stopped, as he ought to have been there before me.

After I had been there about half an Hour, Mr. Daws came; we refreshed our selves, and set off for Concord, to secure the stores, &c. there. We were overtaken by a young Doctor Prescot, whom we found to be a high Son of Liberty. I told him...it was probable we might be stoped before we got to Concord,... I likewise mentioned that we had better allarm all the Inhabitents till we got to Concord; the young Doctor much approved of it, & said, he would stop & would give the more credit to what we said.

We had got nearly half way: Mr. Daws & the Doctor stoped to allarm the people of a House: I was about one hundred Rod ahead, when I saw two men, in nearly the same situation as those officers were, near Charlestown. I called for the Doctor & Daws to come up; —in an instant I was surrounded by four; they had taken down a pair of Barrs on the north side of the Road, & two of them were under a tree in the pasture.

The Doctor being foremost, he came up; & we tryed to git past them; but they being armed with pistols & swords, they forced us in to the pasture; —the Doctor Jumped his Horse over a low stone wall, for that.

When I got there, out started six officers on Horseback, and ordered me to dismount. One of them, who appeared to have the command, examined me, where I came from, & what my Name was? I told him (it was Revere, he asked if it was Paul? I told him yes.) He asked me if I was an express? I answered in the affirmative. He demanded what time I left Boston? I told him; and aded, that There would be five hundred Americans there in a short time, for I had alarmed the country all the way up...

We rode till we got near Lexington Meeting-house, when the militias fired a Voley of Guns, which appeared to alarm them very much. The Major inquired of me how far it was to Cambridge, & if there were any other Road? After some consultation, the Major rode up to the Sargent, & asked if his Horse was tired? He answered him, he was—(He was a Sargent of Grenadiers, and had a small Horse—then, said He, take that man's Horse. I dismounted, & the Sargent mounted my Horse, when they all rode towards Lexington Meeting-house. I went across the burying-ground, & some pastures, & came to the Rev. Mr. Clark's House, where I found Messrs. Hancock & Adams...

Your Humble Servant,
—PAUL REVERE

23.

Ralph Waldo Emerson and the New England Renaissance

Louisa May Alcott's novel *Little Women,* set in the middle of the 19th century, appeared as a movie for the third time in 1994. This enduring story conveys the ambience, architecture and literary awakening of Concord Village.

We see Wayside, the Alcott house in Concord, and the human-scale clapboard and brick houses clustered around it. The mood is not saccharine but serene and moving; the Alcotts as a family are cheerfully bearing the difficulties of living during a bloody Civil War, with gracious response.

Ralph Waldo Emerson put up money for the Alcotts' blessed Wayside as the family struggled financially, buoyed by their faith and mutual support. The children's mother was *a presence.* Their father, Bronson Alcott, who was another reflective thinker, was at war. The actual situation of the Alcotts became the poignant setting of the classic book.

Ralph Waldo Emerson lived his later life largely in Concord in a comfortable white clapboard house that he built for his second wife,

Lidian. This was his home, a crucible of literary blossoming and intellectual independence. During this period the confluence of his Western and Eastern thinking occurred. He became the passionate sage of Concord. He advocated individualism and self-reliance; he was also an activist, a good neighbor, and a loyal and warm family member. Emerson survived terrible personal tragedies with courage. So challenged, he became, on his own, the greatest intellectual adventurer of his age. His enormous influence radiates to this day.

Often, individuals influence the history of a place or a nation more than does a mass movement. We can argue that the three high points of distinguished leadership over 300 years of Concord history were Peter Buckeley in the 17th Century, William Emerson in the 18th Century, and Ralph Waldo Emerson in the 19th Century. The character and power of their contributions in deeds and in words are hard to overestimate. They were giants of their times in many different ways—reflecting deep brilliance on Concord and indeed on New England, and beyond. The common thread running through these three individuals, I believe, is made of character, intelligence and drive.

Ralph Waldo Emerson was ordained and became a ministerial assistant in his father's parish in Boston. He eventually became unsure of the continued drift of dogmatic Calvin church doctrine and the rigid church service. Always a deep, conscientious (and often radical) thinker, he began turning his beliefs toward new waves of thought called transcendentalism and Unitarianism. Followers of these insurgent movements increasingly rejected the strict orthodoxy that Christ *was* God and took a milder position: that Christ was a supreme prophet, at best the son of God. This diverting, independent thought went so far as to hint and then pronounce that each person was a divinity, harboring a God within, and was therefore individually and largely responsible for his or her salvation. The impact views on Calvinist orthodoxy was calamitous.

Ralph Waldo Emerson gave a startling Divinity School Address at Harvard that challenged the existing patterns of religious thought. He was summarily banned by the authorities from preaching anywhere on Sunday. Consequently, he preached on weekdays and concentrated on his essays and his poems. Elsewhere, the reaction in the first half of the 19th century was stunning resistance.

Another more defined and crucial debate was taking place in the forum of Concord and in all of New England, and the rebel Ralph Waldo Emerson was in the thick of it. Historian Van Wyck Brooks summed up the kernel of this new movement as the Great Awakening: "By raising the general estimate of human nature, which the old [Calvinist] religion had despised, [the new American Unitarianism] gave creative life a prodigious impulse..."

Emerson was more persuasive than abrasive in his belief in transcendentalism; he once provided a benign definition of religion: "to love, to serve, to think, and to be humble." For the most part, he was true to this creed.

There is a story that when Emerson was on his deathbed at home in Concord, the parish pastor went to visit him, walking up and down in front of the bed, eyeing the dying man. Finally, the pastor turned toward Emerson and said: "Mr. Emerson, may I inquire of you? Have you, Sir, or have you not, made your peace with the Lord Jesus?"

There was silence.

Slowly, Emerson replied, "I did not know we had quarrelled."

24.
Sudbury Village
Migration from England
to New England

In 1957 a Wesleyan University historian, Sumner Chilton Powell, began a six-year detective hunt among archives and private collections in England and in Massachusetts. His research into arcane and dusty original sources from the 17th-century period (when clerks and clerics wrote in shorthand Latin) resulted in the publication in 1963 of a revealing slice of village history—the transmigration of a community of Puritans from England to a wilderness in the New World to form a village, from scratch that still exists: Sudbury, Massachusetts.

This singular achievement is revealed in *Puritan Village—The Formation of a New England Town* (Sudbury): Wesleyan University Press, 1963. I found a copy of this well-illustrated volume at the Book Mart in Stonington Village—saving me more than six years of the author's exceptional perseverence and frustration. Powell accomplished this feat by doing meticulous research in England to identify and illuminate exactly who arrived in the early 17th century in Sudbury's Indian Territory. This land was too remote and dangerous to have been settled—and an Atlantic Ocean away from the civilized familiarities of 17th century farmlands, long-settled villages and pubs, cheerful church parishes and the prosperous, well-organized wool trading borough of Sudbury, Suffolk.

Powell's study is provocative, shedding light on a hundred-year-old scholarly debate about the origin of the New England village and as the waves of population went westward, of the subsequent villages and towns across America. Sudbury can be considered a true model of how the New England village came about, where the settlers came from, who they were, what they thought about and did, how they disputed and where they went. We can perceive the seeds of democratic development on New World soil and see its severe challenges and desperate travails. We can see, too, the flow of these ideas across America.

Sumner Chilton Powell is wary of generalizations about his subject. He recognizes that there is as much variety as uniformity in village and borough institutions. Emigrants from England tended to form new social groups once they had landed in New England and to "live in settlements considerably apart from one another" so he finds it difficult to believe that they lost "their tendency to be individualistic in attitude and behavior."

The ingenious key to understanding this great transition from England to New England, Powell believes, is a "careful examination of these emigrants who comprised and administered these institutions when they *were* living in England and *again* when they had gathered to form a new town."

The transported Puritans came not from one mold but rather from three distinct types of experience: (1) the open-field manorial village, (2) the bustling, surprisingly advanced incorporated borough of Sudbury, Suffolk, and (3) the enclosed-farm East Anglican village. Yet all of them had a direct relation to the English church parish and a common thread of behavior and attitude, a key factor to keep in mind as we read what happened.

Idealistic leaders of emigration movements face keen, exciting challenges, Powell says: Each early New England village was "a little commonwealth" that was legally "able to select its members and to exclude 'such whose disposition do not suit us, whose society will be hurtful to us.'"★

A major factor in village development in the New World was the grant of freedom for each village to make as many laws as were considered necessary to operate with considerable flexibility in relation to "The Governor and Company of the Massachusetts Bay." Powell's study of Sudbury recognized that for the early years, each village could make an effort to form as much of "an ideal state as its leaders could conceive and find agreement on." The method was joint consensus.

Sudbury is one village whose documentation shows a vivid profile of village contribution to the American ideal of government. This inheritance led, I believe, to the United States Constitution, an amazing political experiment that has lasted longer and perhaps more fruitfully than has any other political experiment in any other nation.

Fortunately, we have a continuity of authenticity. One village clerk dutifully recorded resolutions for Sudbury from its beginning in 1638 until the 1650s, when another clerk took the job and carried on this task until another took the job forward, without break. Documents show the preparatory activities of thirteen of the first selectmen during the period 1600–38 when they were living in England. Powell traced 79 percent of the first grantees of Sudbury.

★John Winthrop, "Declaration in Defense of an Order of Court, 1637." Later incorporated into a General Court order applicable to each village.

All did not go smoothly. Powell recorded a violent dispute in Sudbury from 1655 to 1657. Well documented, it was essentially a battle of the younger, second generation against the constraints imposed by the founders of the village. The founders had set down certain common land "forever." But they soon learned the hard way that the permanency could not hold against a growing, restless, generational population. Land and food; rank and authority. Finally, meeting house debate and vote forced the founders to permit a dissenting group to split off in order that these "younger men", with some "older leaders," might establish another community village to the west, called Marlborough. Powell summarized the situation:

> One might even see the story of early Sudbury as a type of local morality play, replete with Devil, Greed, and Ambition, opposed by both Faith and Prudence. But *personal* Sudbury documents are lacking, and we must leave this drama to the novelist. We can, however, study the remarkable transition of culture and do our best to comprehend the hopeful spirit which kindled these free townsmen. It is a spirit which no New England generation would willingly lose.

Puritan Village focuses on the village leaders, the principal one being Reverend Edmund Brown. Reverend Brown was the brother of Sudbury founder Thomas Brown. They had arrived in the New World together and were two of my ancestors.

Who was Reverend Edmund Brown, and where did he come from? He had been a minister in the borough of Sudbury, Suffolk—northeast of London. Sudbury was known both as a stronghold of

Puritanism in the Eastern Counties and for sending more emigrants to New England than any other town or village in East Anglia. Edmund Brown, Powell said, was probably responsible for the fact that the Massachusetts General Court graced a wilderness settlement with a name which connoted, to the English, "a thriving center of wool manufacture."

Edmund and Thomas were born in Lavenham and Bury St. Edmunds, northeast of Sudbury. Edmund went to Cambridge University and became a member of the Emanuel College at the time of the Nonconformist movement. After graduating in 1624, he returned to Sudbury to assist at one of the larger churches and to continue his studies. He remained in the Sudbury Borough for more than 14 years. There, civic life and church life were intertwined. Brown's experiences there helped influence his decisions in the New World when he was "responsible for helping transplant the vigorous roots of English local government."

Brown was one of three people to petition the General Court of Massachusetts for a village grant, below Concord, on the Musketaquid River. Powell says: "It is very likely that the General Court, full of Emanuel and Cambridge graduates, named the new settlement [Sudbury] in Brown's honor."

The new settlement was situated along the "Great Trail" laid down by centuries of Indians. This combination of paths wound through Massachusetts, into Connecticut, and all the way to what is now Stonington Borough. The new Sudbury—subsequently to be the site of Longfellow's "Wayside Inn"—was not all bleak wilderness. There was a valley, sliced by a great river and devoid of forest, that encompassed a broad plain of meadow grass as high as a man's shoulders. The river was full of salmon, shad, and pickerel; beaver were ever present and busy; there were plentiful wildfowl, grouse, turkeys, bear and deer. While the area was well watered, there would be the continual danger of wolves devastating the village and outer pastures.

In the fall of 1638—at long last—the General Court granted full power to Edmund Brown and his colleagues to "go to their plantation and allot the lands."

Village government at the new Sudbury was not a town theocracy as we have been led to believe. In the rule book, entitled *Body of Liberties,* then debated in the villages of the Bay Colony, Liberty #12 allowed "every man, whether inhabitant or foreigner, free or not free, to come to any town meeting and present any orderly motion." Nonetheless, Powell says, the *Body of Liberties* had a strict definition of a village government: Liberty #66 stated "The freeman of every township shall have power to make such by-laws and constitutions as may concern the welfare of their town...not repugnant to the public laws of the country." It is significant, however, that by "freeman" this early Massachusetts constitution meant "an official church member who has taken an oath to uphold the colony."

The new settlement had much to learn about different human behavior patterns in the wilderness. The village was often confounded by relations with the Indians. There were terrible day and night alerts against sudden attacks by hostile Indians. The new colonists had been used to, and conditioned by, English ways: Paid hands did the dirty fighting; no soldier fought at night, in the snow or in the rain; and no decent soul did battle during the cold of winter or during the harvest season. As Powell relates:

In New England the [villagers] were shocked to hear that there were no rules of warfare that they understood at first. The 'tawney serpents' attacked 'in a monstrous manner' at night, in the rain, during harvests, over the snow,...no accepted civilities; and they seemed as ready to slit the stomach of a pregnant woman as they were to scalp any man who crossed their warpath. The men of Sudbury had to steel themselves for such barbaric tactics. Their [village] was considered an outpost on the frontier, the front line of attack, and their selectmen turned [to the General Court] at Boston for advice on how to proceed.

There is little doubt that Sudbury's and its neighboring villages' organized response to these attacks led to measures of preparation and response that included independent village troops and scouts with arms and powder to blast away, repulse and defeat British Redcoats a century down the road.

There are sometimes silver linings in deep adversity. Without the Indian Wars and sporadic forays against New England villages, the colony could not have, in the opinion of many, succeeded in attaining victory over and independence from the British Crown.

Powell sympathized with the hardships Edmund Brown suffered in the New Sudbury.

Edmund Brown had made many sacrifices to come to Musketaquid valley as pastor of Sudbury's first church. A scholar, a gentleman, a man of wealth, he was also a man of deep religious faith.

But I find his situation not all bad. Edmund Brown had, according to his Will, a house in Sudbury with a "kitchen and a parlor on the first floor, but a study as well, stocked with over one hundred books, folios of music, and his bass viol. [sic] His barn had grain and hay, and below oxen, cows and calves, sheep, pigs, two mares, and a colt. One servant, one maid, and a wife completed the minister's household."

As the 17th century progressed, discontent and a possible arrogance began to spread. Perhaps the extreme danger of the new place began to wear down. Edmund Brown, as Pastor, experienced others disrespect, unheard of in the past. Trouble was brewing in other New England villages, too. (Reverend Peter Buckeley confirmed it in Concord.) Brown's sermons for this period have been lost, but a letter to him from Buckley, dated 1650, reflects the distress of both clergymen. It may be typical of clergy-to-clergy, chief-to-chief correspondence:

> Shall I tell you what I think to be the ground for all this insolvency, which discovers itself in the speech of men?
>
> Truly, I cannot ascribe it so much to any outward thing, as to the putting too much liberty and power into the hands of the multitude, which they are too weak to manage many growing conceited, proud, *self-sufficient,* as wanting nothing. And I am persuaded except there be some means used to change the course of things on this point, our church will grow corrupt day by day, and tumult will arise, hardly to be stilled.

Peter Buckeley's solution was "to make the church doors narrower," that is, "to restrict church membership to those who could be trusted."

The village of Sudbury, founded on "joint consent" was slowly becoming a village of "joint discontent." The basic problem was an insatiable desire for land. The order and rank of the first land distributions were disintegrating. The power of the political selectman over the traditional theological leadership of the pastor was growing wildly; in this dynamic mix of human nature and diversity, a crisis was at hand. The dream of pure harmony and order was coming to an end. The original concept of the meetinghouse as church drifted to become the meeting house as town meeting on secular affairs, centering on "carnal desires" for land and the power of rank. An atmosphere of the mob was prevalent as the second half of the 17th century began.

The younger generation in Sudbury, many landless and disin-franchised, discovered poltical strength at the village meeting-house. Meetings became noisier and angrier. The votes on various issues centered shrilly on who would receive new lands, who could vote, who would be elected to the political office of select-man.

At first Edmund Brown remained aloof to the hard political and economic issues. But as discontent grew he realized he could not, as pastoral leader, waive responsibility for an outcome that could ruin everything for which the original settlers had sacrificed so much. He began to exercise political leadership. This angered the insurgents, affected church attendance and loyalty and led to a dissident leader calling him to task at the meetinghouse, saying directly to him with some venom: "Setting aside your office, I regard you no more than another man."

As Powell summed up the crisis:

The implication is clear. The economic spirit of self-interest, which both Peter Buckeley in Concord and John Cotton in Boston, among others, had feared most, was rapidly spreading in Sudbury. Management and control of land, with consequent administration of [village] affairs, had become the interests and activities which commanded the most intense loyalty among the majority of the

Sudbury inhabitants, and the minister had been bitten by the same desires.

A common method of alternate dispute resolution in New England at the time was to call for a committee of "Reverend Elders" from other village communities to investigate and make resolutions. Brown did so. To the dismay of Sudbury insurgents, the General Court appointed a committee that held several meetings, calling in witnesses and attempting to determine the facts. Essentially, the committee took a conservative position espoused by the Brown contingent—that "every allowed inhabitant" would have the right to pasture animals in the common "according to the acres of meadow he [already] owned..." The committee added, however, that "no one should be able to vote on this issue who was either a noninhabitant or who did not own some meadow acreage." As a last part of their report, the committee concluded that they saw no just ground for the "objection ...and clamorous reports" that had been made against the title to lands held by Reverend Edmund Brown. The report was then submitted to the General Court for ratification.

In the meantime, the offer of investigative assistance from the "Reverend Elders" was rebuffed on the grounds that a majority at Sudbury believed the issues were not church but secular matters, deserving of political resolution at Sudbury's village meetinghouse.

The dispute did not grow to corporal violence, although once "club law" was threatened by a conservative Sudbury leader. Finally, the insurgents with their youthful following petitioned the government in Boston for another grant of land. They would organize a new village community—"another religious and political institution with a different spirit." The result: Sudbury was split asunder. The insurgents were granted generous land farther west to be called Marlborough.

Founder-leader Peter Noyes★ of Sudbury's conservative group was devastated by the rancour and devisiveness that caused the partition of the village. He lost strength; his spirit was broken. Powell wrote that after bequeathing a token of affection to his pastor and "perhaps an implied plea of forgiveness, Peter Noyes left his [village] by the river for the eternal city in his heart."

Concluding his penetrating study of the dramatic events at Sudbury, of its seminal achievements and upheavals, Powell grew somewhat sentimental about "our New England heritage." He said, "The Sudbury [villagers] might not have been able to order their community 'forever' as they hoped, but they set a remarkable example for all the generations which have followed them."†

★Peter Noyes was patriarch of ministerial descendants in New England, e.g. Moses Noyes, Pastor of the Old Lyme, Connecticut church followed by his son and Albert Noyes, Pastor of the First Congregational Church in Stonington, Connecticut. Most leaders in early New England were clergy.

†*Reference:* Edmund Brown, baptized Lavenham, Suffolk 1606 (son of Edm. Brown of this parish); F.L. Weis, *The Colonial* Clergy, *p. 42. Will; Kinsman "John Brown of Bury St. Edmunds, Suffolk: Middlesex Probate, 5/87. Thomas Brown, baptized Bury St. Edmunds, Suffolk; cf. Descendants of Thomas Brown, by G. Brown, pp. 3-6; private papers and geneological records of John Adams Smith Brown, born Worcester, Mass. 1862, died Philadelphia, 1937, and his son George Estabrook Brown, born Philadelphia, 1889, died New York City, 1946.*

25.

Paget Parish
Pristine Village in Bermuda

Based on the crystalline sea,
Of thought and its eternity.

PLATO

In the winter of 1937, my father announced to my mother and the four children, "This summer we're all going to a small village in Bermuda." We had never been outside of the United States, so we were excited. We had lived for ten years (with summers in the Long Island villages of Babylon, Quogue and East Hampton) on a city of concrete, high on Carnegie Hill. There the weather was cold in winter, and air conditionless, hot as hell in summer.

We dreamed of the sentient pleasures awaiting us in just a few months. My father, an organization man, made the plans. Down on the cruise ship *Monarch;* back on the *Queen.* And then a small white cottage up Southcote Road, in Paget Village Parish, seven minutes by foot on soft white coral road to the sea.

On the turbulent voyage south before soothing into the Gulf Stream, all the children threw up repeatedly, undeterred by eating green apples, sipping hot consommé and snacking on dry biscuits out of a tin. My mother, at last free of household chores, threw herself on a starboard deck chair to read Pearl Buck's *The Good Earth.* My father, who had upstaged us by frequent trips to London to search out his ancestors, took refuge in the ship's bar, sipping Scotch and water and deliberately facing the florid barman so as not to perceive the heaving of the sea.

On arrival, we were awake and dressed to view the operatic entrance into Hamilton Harbor. It was punctuated by the petulant roar of the *Monarch,* and answered, quite bravely, by the piping of the two tugs guiding us in to the Furness Front Street Wharf—now jingling, like Babel, with commercial shouts, enthusiastic greetings and unintelligible exclamations. A buzzing Bermudian bazaar.

Now into carriages with kindly drivers wearing white sun helmets, pulled by horses of equal demeanor, we were off with blonde cousin Mignon around the bend at the end of the harbor, alongside the narrow-gauge railroad of lacquered brown and green, clop-clopping faster and faster among bicycles and horse-drawn carts.

In the flash of entry we were inundated with colors never registered before: blues, greens, pinks, yellows, oranges, white-custard roofs and pastels from another world. We rode along the coral roads up serpentine Crowe Hill by artist Birdsy's house, alongside Harmony Hall and down by the village carriage house (now a beauty parlor). Then, to the left, another swing upward, by Saint Paul's Lane, with father imperiously pointing out the slender spire of Saint Paul's Church (of England) to which we were to be involuntarily led on Sunday mornings, then by Marshall's grocery (now Modern Mart & Chicken Delight).

To the right a moment or two after, we came at last to Southcote cottage (sign at the stone-coral gate) and scurried into the low-slung, whitewashed house to claim our summer quarters. Out in five minutes, in swimsuits, running and laughing all the way down to the Elba public beach—for our first memorable dunk in the celebrated azure sea.

Bermuda is a diamond necklace flung on blue-green glass. At one tip are the quaint villages of Saint George's and Saint David's (then a separate island), and at the other lies dream-serene Somerset. There out in the country are lawn tennis, pure white-spired churches and the world's smallest drawbridge, jowled adjacent to the slithering railroad that wends archly to the end of the island.

We saw more of Bermuda in those days than we see today, since World War II that is, because the railroad's cheerful conducters allowed us to swing our bikes onboard and travel the incalculable kilometers to the byways and the ends of the Bermuda earth.

Everyday we explored this seductive necklace island, located incredibly just 500 miles off the North Carolina coast. Bermuda is 145 islands, actually, strung by imperceptible bridges—a puff up of a triple volcano eruption eons ago. It has been struck in a hurricane by the British Ship *Sea Venture* and memorialized forever by Shakespeare in *The Tempest*. Plunk in the middle of the eerie Sargasso Sea, it feels a million beautiful miles from nowhere.

Mark Twain recognized Bermuda as a prelude to heaven. He failed, however, to see it *as* heaven. You understand, he came down frequently on a schooner (as did my grandmother, Miriam Johnson Megargee, a gracious lady with a good posture, on her honeymoon in 1890). Mark Twain used to stay at the old clapboard Princess Hotel on Hamilton Harbor (in town), and sometimes in his final three years at the home of the American Vice Consul Allen (whose teenage daughter apparently fascinated him), but always in the winter season, December to March. After that, white-suited, he would retreat to the banalities of Hartford, Connecticut, to enjoy his white-headed renown as the Supreme Yankee, Samuel Clemens.

One earlier day, riding a steamboat down the Mississippi River to New Orleans, Clemens heard the captain shout, "Mark Twain!" indicating, I suppose, the river water's depth for the safety of the vessel. Clemens liked the authoritative sound of that riverboat exclamation and adopted it straightaway as his own name. But he evidently never felt the passionate spirit inculcated on youthful souls by a visit to Bermuda in the blessed summertime. His loss! He might have have had another *Huckleberry Finn* in another setting.

My brother George—three years older—and I, that sweet summer, used to imagine we were pirates. With spears in hand, noses and shoulders raw with sunburn, glass masks and flippers in tow, we would swim out off Elba Beach to an amber-rusted wrecked ship, inside the reef. There in the spooky stillness of light and shadow, waving coral plants about us, we discovered, not treasures of gold and silver, but rather two remarkable moray eels—each four glistening feet long—one green and one black. Slithering in a corner of the captain's cabin, now deep under water, they fascinated us with their catlike grins, exhibiting to our combined pleasure and horror innumerable sharp needle teeth. It was macho in those salad days to poke the vicious morays until our bursting lungs compelled return to the surface for gasps of air, after which we would return for more mischief. Before the summer was over, my brother had lost his best front tooth in a struggle with me underwater at the wreck—now gone forever.

The magical reefs, the magnificent under-sea world, sparkling with the polish of the radiant sun, provided daily eight-hour voyages of wonder. We made friends with Disney-like fish: 605 species in these waters including grouper, chub, wahoo, marlin, tuna, dolphin, bonefish and amberjack, as well as the frightened flickering silversides. The parrot fish were more predictable than the moray eels, less tricky and explosive than Bobby the Barracuda, who whisked around off Coral Beach midway to the ominous big reef where more than rumor told of man-biting sharks, lurking sullenly for a feast of young sun-cooked flesh.

Considering the time George and I spent underwater, sometimes led by Malcolm Van Dyke Martin and John Webber Hornburg, it is not surprising that we came upon a shark or two. With utter naive adventurism we would pursue them, haughtily, in the fashion of the Light Brigade, armed with our clumsy, rusted spears. We never once speared a shark or caught a barracuda.

Returning to Bermuda and its incomparable parish communities many times over the years, our eyes observed the changes and the changeless as well. We noticed the sale of the gracious railroad to Paraguay for a cargo of Argentine beef and a case of Johnny Walker Black Label; we suffered the paving of the inimitable coral back roads in the name of progress; then the arrival of ubiquitous small automobiles like ants across a barn door, affecting the culture and romance of the Impressionistic idyll so loved by Winslow Homer.

Gone were the *Monarch* and the *Queen,* sacrificed to World War II as troop carriers; gone were the little, hot grocery stores along the south shore roads: canned goods, green-bottled beer with a neat label in sharp black and red, "Brauerei Beck & Co.—Bremen, Germany—Beck's Bier," but no ice for Cokes or beer, yet always an enormous wheel of English cheese, like a millstone, covered by an opaque glass cover with a knob. The rich smell of the steaming cheese escaped from around the cover and fetidly filled the store with an earthiness remembered a half-century later as if yesterday.

My vivacious sisters, Harriett and Bebe, were sufficiently thrilled with the romance of the dulcet Bermuda breezes, the soft colors, lapis lazuli sea, and sweet flowering trees, that they became receptive to the ardent pursuits of various American and Bermudian swains. One was an English-trained architect, who is still a bit active on the island today. Another was a blond graduate of Yale whom my father introduced slyly as the captain of the Yale varsity crew "defeated at Henley." The fellow responded to this dig with the droll insouciance "aha ..." uttered by James Stewart in the Philip Barry movie *Philadelphia Story.*

In those days, romance was triggered in the glorious outdoor, hotel dancing pavilions in Paget Parish. In huge concrete leafs, twelve-piece orchestras played waltzes, fox trots and sambas to the delight of light-footed elbow-jerking young couples, she with deep dips and dresses like lampshades; he with Vasolined hair, white pants and, if very preppy, red yacht slacks.

Demanding to know precisely where his daughters were spending the evening with their boyfriends, my father would suggest to me that we pay an investigatory visit to the open-air dancing palaces at Elbow Beach Hotel, Inverurie or Belmont. Riding like commandos on bicycles over the cool coral roads, the black sky drawn with geometric designs, my father in white hunter's helmet and Bermuda shorts, we would sneak up on the band-ignited revelers and try to identify my sisters, whom they were with, what they were doing and, more especially, whether they had limited themselves to Coca-Cola or, at the outside, claret and lemonade. We rarely, if ever, discovered perfidy and would return silently the way we had come to Southcote. And so to bed.

There were endless energetically planned family trips to Devil's Hole, the Perfume Factory, the Crystal Caves, underwater thrills at Harrington Sound, the Aquarium to photograph sand sharks and moray eels, Saint David's lighthouse, over to and up the steps of cast-iron Gibbs light overlooking Waterlot Inn where my father took me alone one day to meet raconteur restaurateur Claudia Darrell with her red hair flying; she told us a hundred lurid tales of the island (some of them true); to Hamilton City to shop—Trimingham's, H.A.&E. Smith, A. S. Cooper, the book store, century-old Bluck's, Gosling Brothers (Black Seal rum), over to the esteemed Twenty-One Bar, overlooking the cruise ships—very smart to be there, my oldest sister insisted. "Everyone is *here*," she said, sipping a dark rum and Coca-Cola.

Ferries cobwebbing the places to go and to visit. Discussions as to whether the place was worth seeing but, as Samuel Johnson discerned, was it worth *going* to see? Bike trips to the village of Saint George's (my father loved history, and here it was). "Look, Peter, this church [reading] was established in 1727. *Can you imagine that?*" he would ask. "No, I can't," I would respond.

Back in late afternoon, we pushed our bikes uphill under firecracker bowers of poinciana trees, the birds shrieking and the roads dusty with beige in the denouement of the long day. The climate is cozy and warm. Evening is sensed in the rise of the breeze, but not before my father had an enterprising idea for all of us. "Why don't we scoot into Hamilton for a cool moment in the Quarry Bar?"

No one dissented, for we knew that, high on Hamilton hills, there was a special place—200 feet below street level, 300 steps below, cut in coral stone, a quarried-out bar, cool-as-a-cucumber, in hospitable cedar wood. And there, bless the owner, was cold German beer, cold

Coca-Cola, cold lemonade and a moment of peace to contemplate the day. Until my mother, long disenchanted with Quarry Bar's gloomy ambience, would say, "Well, let's go home to Southcote." We then took our bikes on the ferry from the spot where policemen in helmets at midday directed traffic of carriages, carts and dignified bicyclers. The carriage horses wore straw hats. Everyone wore hats in those days of 1937, when the Japanese sank the U.S.S. *Panay* and isolationism was at its peak.

The day had ended, yes, but not its joyous counterpart—the jeweled nighttime, as lovely and as exciting as the day. At Elbow Beach in Paget Parish, Eddie Wittstein and his Yale Prom Orchestra played "I Dreamt That I Dwelt in Marble Halls" and "The One O'clock Jump." The sounds drifted up, feathered by the soft rising and falling of the wind. Crickets creaked in rising crescendo.

After experimentation as meticulous as a research physician's, my father finally settled on Gosling's Black Seal rum as his favorite evening toddy on the Southcote terrace, overlooking a garden now gone to seed. His digestive system had been insensibly destroyed on the New York Stock Exchange where he had a seat but never sat. October, 1929, and the subsequent dreary downgrading Depression years had taken their livid toll of his vascular system. So he was naturally delighted to discover that Bermuda's Gosling Black Seal rum brought incomparable euphoria to an anxious and beleaguered spirit. He hit upon a plan to import a case or two to New York and in this way carry Bermuda's grace and well-being directly to his home environment on Carnegie Hill in New York City. The rum was duly delivered. For the next week or so he sampled and tippled his treasure, but, alas, once back among the bears in the dreadful Stock Exchange on Wall Street, his old suffering returned, despite the medicinal Black Seal in the library closet.

———

Half of life is memory. It is not a chronological video, good and bad flickering on screen. It is, I think, edited patches and flashes, recollections as sudden and precise as the prick of a pin. We dream much of it. How satisfying, how truly marvelous to have had, by sheer luck, that special summer in a pristine village in Bermuda, at a distant time. Regular visits—the latest in the summer of 1996—rekindle the memories. The sweetness and the colors remain.

To the visitor from Carnegie Hill, where I continue to live, Bermuda is still an exquisite sanctuary, sheltered pridefully by an Olympian-minded government and warm-hearted people. The place where we stayed in 1937 (and where I am again rewriting this retrospection) was the Parish Paget Village area of Coral Beach and Elba on the incomparable south shore. It is still a perfect antidote for city drears. All six senses (the sixth is appreciation) attest to it.

Our family, *new* generations, come back again to savor, to remember and to enjoy. We read; we write; we love.

The tooth rock still stands at the end of Coral Beach; the bird's-eye cat-bird cedar table is up on a terrace; the curved, turreted lookout provides 180 degrees of rare seascape bathed in light and painted pale blue. Palms sway over us with dignity, dressed in stripped skins of rough brown-grays, against the background of red-veined bay grape leaves, undulating lazily over Persian azure seas.

Out beyond is the cold cobalt waters where hazy tankers roam. Just as always, the waves, protected by the reefs, slip in to the shoreline to curtsy and retreat. These gentle waves of white embroidery do not crash or thunder as in Maine, East Hampton, Mantoloking and Portugal. They glide in as waves do in a ballet, with grace, murmuring to us of peace and holiday.

The clouds in Paget are still English clouds—up high, moving or stationary (Arabic writings) across the horizon, often sprinkled with cinnamon, and escorted by puffy pilots in gray. These of course were painted there long ago by Constable at another serene time. Contrasted in texture into three deep dimensions, somehow transposed by the Greek light and the heavenly repose.

The pink sands are still for children, and grandchildren, not conducting the heat of the strong summer sun. Bermudians love their natural blessings of small-scale village communities, ocean, flowers and sky. Their silken voice tones reflect calm and gratitude for this special spirit of place.

The changes of so-called modern progress have not diminished or sullied the pristine parish-village of Paget and the neighboring communities. Today you would hardly notice the substitution of small cars for the sleek railroad. Coral Beach is there in all its natural glory. The people are still welcoming and kind. The constrained wise government sees to it that the total environment *is* protected, that commerial enroachment is deterred, that neons and billboards are banned and that the extraordinary quality of life that has endured for many generations is maintained. Incredibly, there is no place you could walk or drive in all of Bermuda that is not serene and clean.

In your own village odyssey, you should not miss the savor of Bermuda, and particularly, I think, the village Parish of Paget on the south shore.

26.

Villages of Greece
Yesterday and Today
The Echoes of
4,000 Years of History

A summer visit our family made to the Greek Mediterranean and numerous Greek villages is as entrancing in our memories as it was at the time, twenty years ago. Here's how it happened.

Alexandra and I wanted to take the three children still at home— Nathaniel (thirteen), Alexandra II (eight) and Brooke (five)—to explore the Mediterranean basin of our civilization and discover spiritual roots. We wished to experience, to feel, Greece's intimate villages on foot, its Aegean islands as well as the ancient cities of Alexandria and Cairo, and to end up, quietly, on the island of Corfu in the Ionian Sea, off the boot of Italy, for a final rest and reflection before returning to the contrast of New York City.

We shared a notion, discussed many times before we went, that a family visit to this time-capsule cradle of world history would provide insights for all of us about life's meaning, about how to sustain our spirit over the years and about how, perhaps, to contemplate the purpose of life on earth and beyond.

"Other countries may offer you discoveries in manners or love or landscape," said novelist Lawrence Durrell, "Greece offers you something harder—the discovery of yourself."

We gathered the three children around us one evening in New York and set down the terms of our travel to Greece. First, everyone would keep a diary (tangible memory)—every day—no falling behind! Second, everyone would be helpful, cheerful, travel lightly (one suitcase each) and not get sick. By the grace of the Lord, this plan worked out, and everyone kept notebooks about the holiday, legible enough to detail the reaction of each of the five (ages 53 years to five) to our experiences. I came across the diaries one day, tucked away in a drawer in the library. My mind exploded with the recollections of Greece as vivid and colorful as yesterday's.

Looking back, I think that what we found was not so much discovery of the meaning of life as something Joseph Campbell termed the "experience of being alive." As he would say, we heard a little of the song of the universe and the music of the spheres—"music we dance to even when we cannot name the tune."

An advertisement in *The New York Times* had seduced us to make the trip together. We were told, in luring copy, that Greece was 1,417 golden islands basking in warm sun, where we could marvel at the "towering Parthenon bathed in the silvery Athenian moonlight" and hear the "echoes of 4,000 years of history."

Brooke's first diary entry:
Mommy had shown me pictures of Greece before we came. I was most excited about going on the big boat. I thought Greece would

have white stone houses, blue blue blue blue blue sky and blue blue blue blue *blue* water. The sun will be big and bursting and yellow and shining.

Greece and the Mediterranean became a unique, exciting experience in a three-week, non-package dash through history. The trip had a curious and perhaps permanent impact on our lives. I have tried to figure out the reason for the magnetism of the Mediterranean on a family living 5,000 miles away. Many indescribable things happened. It was a journey through time. For even the youngest, history—so dry and uncompromising—became alive, exciting.

We climbed the Acropolis and touched the Parthenon; swam in a translucent blue bay in sight of the magnificent Temple to Poseidon at the village of Sunion; ate truly vine-ripened tomatoes, skewered lamb and veal washed down with lemonade or fresh Domestica wine; entered the Queen's private apartment in the Palace of Knossos in northern Crete; patted the five-foot thick fortifications of the Knights of Saint John at Rhodes; saw with new eyes the dawn come up at sea and the sun set from the looming islands; sat at outside café tables in small, white-faced villages while life throbbed around us; looked, bedazzled, at the cliffs of Santorini, the dignified coastlines and the incomparable wine-dark sea. You feel Greece. It is a sensual place.

After a trip through Egypt's port city, Alexandria, we arrived four hours later on a bus in 104-degree heat at Cairo's Egyptian Museum. We were hot and tired. All five of us had long loved the sea; if we had a choice we preferred to be at the water's edge.

The children were disenchanted to go into a dark and dusty

museum, almost dreary to look at—sticks and stones and broken old bones and mummies. Brooke pleaded, "Do we have to?" It was crowded and the visiting group was large. Yet each of us responded to the unique riches inside: Tutankhamen's exquisite treasures, elaborate death masks and objects from inside his tomb, so refined and detailed that Alexandra said she thought modern designers had repeatedly borrowed all that is true and beautiful—purity of line and form—from early Egyptian discoveries. There were so many fine objects we observed—a comb, a slingback chair, jewelry, blind hinges—imagine, more than 3,000 years ago! (Later we learned that the corn found in the tomb still can be popped today.)

Within a year or so, these same precious objects, with elaborate fanfare, were transported to the Metropolitan Museum of Art in New York City for a bombastic show, clean and well lit. The lines of people outside waiting to get in were endless. It interested me that the children, their appetites whetted, seemed more excited about the treasures' New York presentation than seeing them in Cairo.

When we arrived aboard our ship at the Greek island of Rhodes, Alexandra's one entry was:

In the Greek world Rhodes is as far southeast from Corfu as you can get. These waters are clear greens merging into blues, foam lit with phosphorescence from within.

We walked through time. The 15th-century old city with pebbled streets of the Knights of Saint John stirred our imagination of long long ago.

My diary reflects a scene in Crete:
Most exciting see of Crete is the Palace of Minos at Knossos; its discovery was a wonder event of the 20th century. Sir Arthur Evans, an English gentleman, gave himself and his fortune to a controver-

sial restoration—reconstruction of fallen parts, restoration of frescoes and sculptures. By careful reconstruction he gave to the visitor today a more vivid picture of how royalty lived in the heyday
of ancient Crete. This civilization continued for a thousand years.

The palace lies a few moments south of the mid-north city of
Heraklion where we docked on schedule at 10 a.m. The Palace
stands atop a small hill, Kefaia, above the banks of a river dry in
summer but large enough for transportation to the town. The view
from the Palace is comparable to the center valley of Corfu—
cypresses, green and straight up, olive trees galore (it was an olive
grove Sir Arthur had to buy out) and graceful rolling vineyards.

Difficult to believe that surrounding this Palace was the capital
city of Crete harboring a population of more than 100,000. Homer
sang of 90 cities of Crete. Today archeologists have uncovered more
than 100, which of course proves that Homer was incapable of
exaggeration. None of these cities had a wall. Sea power was sufficient for protection. Crete maintained the peace for a millennium
in the Aegean, from which flowered unprecedented prosperity and
art.

A major reason Crete prospered more than other Aegean islands
during the Minoan period was its active trade with Egypt. Going
to Alexandria and to Cairo helped us fit together some of the puz-
zling pieces of the Mediterranean past.

About 1700 B.C. the Palace was destroyed by a stunning blow,
most likely an earthquake caused by eruption of the Santorini
(Thera) volcano named Thiria. Out of the horrendous destruction
a new indomitable civilization grew up, more beautiful and
stronger than ever, a harbinger of the Hellenic classical civilization,
and in turn we hope our own.

To an ordinary family of five living in an apartment in
Manhattan, an on-foot inspection of the Minoan Palace is so exciting because the restoration lets you step into the apartments themselves—windows and balconies overlooking a magnificent view;

ingenious passages and staircases; carefully planned shafts of light as well as openings to regular breezes for constant air conditioning; a drainage system envied by architects today; drinking water conduits and those for washing, as well, showed fastidiousness unrecognized in many new places. The drinking water came from a hill above, ultimately by aqueducts; the apartments we saw were decorated in such vivid colors as Pompeian red. We were surprised to find relentless color on the outside columns, although the pillars were amber and black.

Communication yet privacy, shelter yet a grand view, simple lines yet spectacular stateliness all combine to make us see for ourselves that the Palace of Knossos more than 3,000 years ago was one of the finest buildings ever known, in an incomparably picturesque surrounding.

Unlike Egypt and the existing Greek world, here was architecture dedicated quite realistically to the service and joy of man.

Alexandra II (age eight):
Santorini used to be round, but a gigantic volcanic eruption cut it in half and one part fell into the sea forever! Now there is a cliff one thousand feet straight up. We landed there in a small fishing boat. We took a donkey ride up to the top of the hill while all the way up I was saying how mean it was for the donkey to spend his time taking fat heavy people up with no rest! One thousand feet! Well, we got up the hill, went shopping and had some ice cream and walked down. When we got down, I looked all the way up at the white houses.

Peter (father):
Sea Voyage to Santorini (Thera). Suddenly, our boat entered a blue-green gulf and we were flat up against a menacing cliff rising

straight up 1,000 feet from a tiny port. At the top peeping over was a white string of houses, churches, shops and the proud Hotel Atlantis. The earthquake of 1450 B.C. was an unparalleled catastrophe, devastating neighboring islands as well as destroying the first flower of the Minoan empire in Crete 70 miles away (when the volcano exploded, the middle of the island sank; the sea rushed in, to be spurted out in a historic tidal wave across the whole Aegean Sea).

In 1967 archeologists dug into a Bronze-Age town of 30,000 souls and found three-story buildings and houses that had been paralyzed in lava ash before the final explosion. Found within were extraordinary frescoes of plants, birds, people, fish—and antelopes and apes. Some experts think these frescoes surpass all those of the Mediterranean including Egypt's.

"The island is officially called Thira (Thera), but mostly known as Santorini, from its patroness, Saint Irene of Thessalonika.

Typical Greek mythology. "Delos is the birthplace of the twins Apollo and Artemis, whose mother, Leto, was relentlessly pursued by the serpent Python, by the order of Hera, the jealous wife of Zeus, by whom she was pregnant."

Alexandra I (mother):

Walking through the maze of narrow whitewashed streets, getting lost in the labyrinth of bright dazzling light reflected against the blue-white light is the charm of the small village on Mykonos. Walking up to the hill of windmills with their white triangular sails and seeing them spinning around in the summer winds is a joy.

We sat at an open café on the waterfront and watched the people. Mykonos wasn't crowded at all for an August Sunday. Our lunch was on the waterfront, and we had shrimp, eggplant salad and vine leaves. It was earthy and beautiful. We hopped down another street for our Greek salad and our first taste of retsina. I would drink retsina again only if I were dying and was told this potion was my only help for a few more moments of life. There is nothing enjoyable about the taste of turpentine. Henry Miller drank it when he was in Greece in the early '40s but cautioned to drink it with a full meal of lamb and eggplant and bread.

Nathaniel (age fourteen):

As we walked up we noticed a very nice restaurant that had a delicious Greek menu written on a wooden plaque. We sat and waited for service. We attracted attention and got some lunch—fresh shrimp with no formaldehyde and roasted chicken and spit-grilled lamb. What a meal, with a salad of dark red tomatoes and Greek olives.

We moved on for our dessert at a neighboring restaurant so we could see and feel more. We ordered three watermelons and one bottle of white wine. My dad wasn't particular in Greece. He bought us delicious watermelon and a bottle of retsina which is a wine with retsin in it and it tastes like old sneakers. We all read that it was terrible, but now we know it is terrible.

We moved on and passed a bakery where a man was making bread. We smelled the sweet aroma and poked our heads into the small shop, but after a second of heaven the old bakerman yelled: "No bread, no bread!" We retreated—walking back the way we came and had ice cream for three in a small café out on the waterfront. We sat in front of abrightly colored fishing boats, people passing by and thinking of the days to come.

After coming back through Athens we took an airplane for the trip to the Greek Island of Corfu, dotted with village life.

Peter:

A swing to the northwest from Aegean to Ionian, there is a special place near the heel of Italy but separated absolutely from brooding Albania—Corfu, an emerald scimitar surrounded by translucent seas and brilliant light, flushed with constantly changing colors of mother-of-pearl. I found this idyllic island (favorite of Lawrence Durrell) smelling of watermelon, cool and freshly cut.

Alexandra I (mother):

Lawrence and Gerald Durrell say this island is flawless. For years I've dreamed about coming here—not for a boat stopover but to take a house, to unpack and, at least until a reasonable length of time has slipped by unhurried, to be. To be, to live in Corfu: my fantasy.

I hear nothing but the sea which is drowning out the buzz of insects and the slight chirping of birds. Evening is here in a soft transition. The sun fades taking the blue. The sky and water have a mist and pale quality—a softness in preparation for eventual darkness and rest.

We have been blessed with a moon for our entire stay in Greece. I am afraid tonight we will have to remember what the glow was like all these nights we dined with the moon glowing the darkened sea in a dazzling shimmer of diamonds moving, breathing, living with us each night.

We see the razor-thin new moon, like a scimitar the Greeks used to cut ground cover.

When we were in Athens, we could see the pale pink cast of the white marble of the buildings on the Acropolis come alive by this light and on each island we went to—each evening on board looking at the flickering Aegean Sea we were followed by this expanding circle. Now we must remember the moon as it was. I will keep it in my mind until we leave."

Peter (father):

Water colors—Aegean and Ionian seas. Deep throbbing emerald; laser nitric green; seas of turquoise; sapphire at noon; golden pretzels of fractured sunlight dazzling the sandy bottom of the shore through prisms of pure water.

Greek summer climate: 70-90 but without the humidity of the Caribbean or Bermuda.

Corfu: an island of eternal spring. Lush green island bathed in lilac light, washed by seas of emerald blue; shaded from piercing sun by battalions of gnarled olive trees, centuries old. Across is Albania and mainland Greece—a backdrop in stunning contrast to Corfu: barren, brooding and dark.

Alexandra I (mother):

This literal paradise, this isolated faraway island, lush and dripping with a flow of nature, surrounded by the Ionian Sea, which strokes the shore in rhythmic pulsebeats, is extraordinarily beautiful. I'm here living in a house a few yards from this moving film of sky and water. Our bed faces the sea, and the only thing that separates me from a perfect canvas of sea and heaven is occasionally my toes get in the way.

This island has a spirit of place, as Lawrence Durrell would say. Corfu is life seen through a looking glass where every mirror of beauty, all the flowering fruit trees, juicy figs, dignified olive trees, arrogant shafts of cypress, lush greens contrasting gently against the kaleidoscope of seafoam blues, greens, purples and powder-soft blue sky would be seen through unscratched lens, dust free, in focus with lighting brighter and clearer and sunnier, happier than any you've ever experienced.

Corfu's elegant architecture in the village is Venetian. Proud, slim shuttered houses hug each other in a pleasing jumble along narrow alleys, with striking colonnades running along them. A fine mixture of Greek and Bermudan colors abound—Spanish melon, sienna, umber, pistachio, tawny yellow, all set off in style with light-headed rococo grillwork and balconies sufficient perhaps for a small cat. This classic village surrounds with generosity the largest square in Europe—the magnificent Spianada, protected by two soldier-boy forts reminiscent of Rhodes to the east at the other end of the Greek world.

Peter (father) diary entry:
Back to our house—one night after dinner of moussaka and souvlaki, across the black of the sea we were startled by seven glaring lights several miles off the southeast coast toward Albania and mainland Greece. The night and sea were still, and the fat moon was reluctant to rise. From fishing boats huge carbide flares lured fish to the nets. We discussed among ourselves the morality of attracting fish to their doom at night by artificial lights. Brookie pondered this problem for a moment. "I think it is unfair—I think it is unfair—especially for the fishes…"

My diary has notes on the old Corfu village area of Kerkyra, at Corfu's center:

Weathered plaster of the 18th-century houses, allowed to go cracked umber, yet shuttered and regal. Wash out on the line, sometimes all across the narrow street. By our observing the laundry out to dry, each occupant of the dwelling is revealed. Even the most modest housing has in the windows balconies and niches, pots of geraniums, impatiens or greens. Pounding light floods the darkest spaces. Children play; men and women sell, trade and craft leather, wood and stone.

Aegli is a spirited restaurant under the colonnades: typically good in the delicious dishes of the island. You cannot help marveling at the tomatoes, aubergine, fruit and random service that extends down and up the colonnades and at waiters dodging traffic across the street to the esplanade. These facile waiters are alert and resourceful, full of bravado and not beyond serving you while at the same time nudging and addressing a passing blonde girl, who circles back on the opposite side.

Alexandra II:
I love Corfu with fresh air and narrow streets and beautiful flowers. One day we went into town and went into a bakery shop. We saw beautiful pastries. We asked what was what and found one we liked: it was an apple pastry. It was hot—and well I just can't spit the words out—well, it was super duper! Then we had lunch and a beautiful day.

Alexandra I:
I am lounging at the edge of the water. Across from me is Albania to the northeast and Greece to the southeast about 18-20 miles away. There is a mountain as sandy and dry as the pyramids in Giza that looks as though Brookie had gotten her watering can and rounded all the sharp edges. Across this living sea of blues bathed in mysterious light is a barren rocky land.

Here in eyesight is a thick healthy hedge of morning glories which are strong peacock blue in the morning and fade to lavender blue in the afternoon as they prepare to close for the evening.

Under all the olive trees is a ground cover called Aphrodite's hair which is singularly pea pod in shape and reaches out toward the water and sun.

At the north end of our house is a garden filled with yellow, orange, pink, purple and red zinnias and *Astrickia* (small stars) with their lacy-thin petals in pinks and purples with yellow happy faces. We have fresh flowers in our rooms, even the bathrooms. The girls are in special charge of picking flowers and changing the water each day.

On the west side of our house we have a tangerine tree, lemon trees with white blossoms, one of which bears "ugly" type fruit, orange trees, prune trees, a peach tree, and down the path leading to our house, which is the farthest away from people of all the houses on the water here, there is a pale pink oleander with fine pinwheel leaves and peppermint centers, darker pink oleanders, jasmine, fan palm, bamboo, hibiscus.

The middle of our tawny yellow house is open to the sky and has been given over to a regal olive tree, proudly there for 500 years. Each bedroom looks directly east over the Ionian Sea with a columned terrace in front of sienna shutters.

On this side of the island there are pebbles instead of sand at the water's edge. Despite love for the white sandy beaches of the Caribbean, I find these smooth egg-shaped stones fascinating. Alexandra II and Brooke have made a collection of tile chips, fitting them together like a mosaic—most discovered underwater or washed ashore. Corfiot workmen throw them to sea when they are finished tiling a bathroom! Colored treasures under water.

From prior trips to Greece I have brought back tiny smooth pebbles and put them in silver cigarette boxes to be rubbed in hand and examined. Each one demands special attention. Yesterday, Brooke found a stone with a portrait of a cocker spaniel. A child's treasure!

The second-highest mountain on Corfu is Aghios Dimetrios; it is about three miles south and swings like an arm east. We all see a lady in the mountain lying down after a too-big lunch, and her highest peak reaches up about 600 M (3'3" per meter).

Because it is so clear I feel as though I could reach over and touch the mountaintop, but when I study it with binoculars, I see in detail whole villages and fields of olive groves and the entire green curving blanket broken up in horizontal harmony by armies of marching postured cypress trees taller and more energetic than the bending twisted irregular olive trees. Cypress trees are definitely human—they are a whole lot more reserved and rigid than their neighbors.

Olive trees spread out their trunks from the roots up and grow in a freedom determined by the environment in which they were planted. The Venetians gave ten gold pieces to Corfiots who planted an olive grove of a hundred trees. Then there were more than two million trees and today more than three and a half million. When planted on a hill they grow toward the sea—light and air so they reach at all angles disregarding the purely vertical position of the cypress.

The trunk of an olive tree is elephant-like with wrinkles and a gray leathery appearance—pitted with holes. When you drive through an olive grove you see the blue-green sea and sky beyond through many of the tree trunks which are opened as views from one side of the trunk through to the other.

As I sit writing, the waves are folding over and over, freshly bringing this salty clear water to my attention, saying gently—come, come, swim.

Small black olives are dropping from the tree right on me every few minutes as the wind moves their silver leaves. Olive tree leaves are small (about 1" to 1.5" long on an average) and they are always being twisted around by the wind. The tops of the leaves are actually a strong green color, but it is the bottoms which are pale and silver which lend the magical silver shimmer to the groves.

I am at my desk facing the water. There is a breeze flowing freshness from the front of our house where the fruit trees are to the back of the house. A few fishing boats pass by. In front of me is a Corfu pottery vase holding a few dozen bows of pink shooting-star flowers, reaching in all directions. Their skinny bending petals look as if they were made of crepe paper and cut into hundreds of strips. Jasmine is mixed in for fragrance, and the palest pink-white blossom stands out against such a mass of pink. I always have fresh flowers on my writing desk wherever I am—one fresh flower is enough—even if it is a fallen blossom otherwise unappreciated.

Being in Greece is to see everything reborn—fresh. Nothing is too big or too small to appreciate. Because the light is so perfect, you can see thirty miles of coastline and, from the same perspective, see an olive tree above you. Take one small branch and study each leaf and olive, glance at the soft aqua sea below and under the rippling quiver study the pebble candy beneath—pebbles all look delicious— caramels and nuggets and candy-coated almonds.

As the diaries of the five of us wound down on our preparation for returning to New York, Alexandra I commented: "The only sadness about our trip ending is that we know it can never be duplicated, and in our quest for new experiences, we won't even try to. This is the sadness—the page being turned and suddenly you realize that that was the last word in the book. That period ended your journey."

I like to ask all those who have made the voyage to the Greek island villages with their flowers and perfume, "What did you experience?"

Greece is always the same. *Sublime.*

PART FOUR

I

I want it said of me by those who knew me best—that I
always plucked thistle and planted a flower where I thought a
flower would grow.

ABRAHAM LINCOLN

II

I must study politics and war, that my sons may
have the liberty to study mathematics, philosophy, geography,
natural history, navigation, commerce
and agriculture...in order to give their children a right to
study painting, poetry, music, architecture, statuary, tapestry and
porcelain.

JOHN ADAMS,
(in a letter to his beloved Abigail)

III

The mind is its own place, and in itself
Can make a heaven of hell, a hell of heaven.

JOHN MILTON
PARADISE LOST

IV

A man must have a share in the passions and actions of his
time, at the peril of being judged not to have lived.

JUSTICE OLIVER WENDELL HOLMES

V

Here's Death, twitching my ear:
"Live," says he, "for I'm coming."

—VIRGIL
(quoted on the radio by Justice Oliver Wendell Holmes
on his 90th birthday in 1931)

VI

It is up to us to haul ourselves out of the slough of Despond.
We must act. We must cultivate our garden.

VOLTAIRE,
CANDIDE

VII

To see a world in a grain of sand,
And a heaven in a wild flower.
Hold infinity in the palm of your hand,
And eternity in an hour.

WILLIAM BLAKE
THE SMILE

27.

Carnegie Hill
Village in the City

Carnegie Hill—on the upper east side of Manhattan—is an example of a microcosm of the vintage village in the middle of a vast sky-scrapered metropolis, renowned since the Dutch put a trading post on its point in 1625, calling it New Amsterdam; sheltered from the Indians and the British by a high wall on what is now Wall Street.

Here to New Amsterdam came early refugees to the New World. Among them was a forebear, Sarah de Rapalyée, enciente on the voyage on the *Nieuw Amsterdam* from Holland. The de Rapalyée family were desperate Huguenot refugees from Brittany, not far from Quimper. Trade-oriented Holland was tolerant of hounded religious Protestants. In its harbors Dutch ships flew flags with red and white stripes, which were adopted by Betsy Ross for the new America in 1776 in appreciation of such symbol of liberty.

On Carnegie Hill, city people in the 20th century have enjoyed human-scale attributes of village life: self-contained small residences, churches, synagogues (and one new mosque at 96th Street), shops, entrances to Central Park for bicycling and walking around the picturesque reservoir; a literal mile of museums, little restaurants and cafés, primary and secondary schools, health facilities, scattered libraries, improvement associations of merit such as Carnegie Hill Neighbors.

Since 1981, Carnegie Hill Neighbors has addressed all quality-of-life issues on Carnegie Hill, orchestrating visual village face lifting in year-round trees, flowers, architecture, and constraints on wild development. The designation by the New York Landmarks Preservation Commission in 1974 of much of the area as the Carnegie Hill Historic District assured retention of handsome buildings and the vitally essential human scale of this quiet residential neighborhood.

More than 400 fine old houses and other buildings are now either designated New York City Landmarks or are within the Carnegie Hill Historic District. Much of this extraordinary uplift to the environment is due to Fred Papert, Ronald Spencer and especially Elizabeth Ashby, who have worked hard as leaders to see to it that essential harmonious changes are made and maintained.

Carnegie Hill is bounded on the west by Fifth Avenue, on the east by the west side of Third Avenue (once the Boston Post Road), on the north by East 98th Street, and on the south by East 86th Street. Shortly before Andrew Carnegie made his fortune in steel, Park Avenue and Fifth Avenue were dirt roads.

When I first came to live on Carnegie Hill in September, 1927, at age five, the area had recently blossomed as a village community, separated if not isolated from the central city by East 86th Street to the south and 96th Street and Park Avenue to the north. Slowly, the Grand Central railroad had been sunk along Park Avenue until, by the mid twenties, island malls, encased by iron fences, green grass and ventilation grills, covered the electrified trains grinding back and forth underground.

But this beautification of the new Park Avenue extended only to 96th Street, aesthetically limiting the contours of Carnegie Hill village. All villages seem to be somehow enclosed and clustered. Our biological sense, centuries old, responds to this enclosed, comforting integrity. Maybe, the security of the womb. Better a natural, free enclosure than the closed-in, gated community, the current trend across America.

Before steel-industry giant Andrew Carnegie (barely 5 feet 2 inches tall) in his retirement built his Georgian mansion at Fifth Avenue on a block between 90th Street and 91st Street (now the Smithsonian design museum), the area looked like a moonscape. Squatters in shanties had to be shooed off before Carnegie could start building his palazzo.

A riding academy was originally located across 90th Street on Fifth Avenue, then tennis courts, now the Episcopal Church of the Heavenly Rest. It was constructed in time for the opening service on Easter, March 31, 1929 (our family huddled in the balcony) which was led by the ebullient Henry Darlington, D.D. He was succeeded by rectors John Ellis Large, D.D., J. Burton Thomas, D.D., Reverend Alanson Houghton and Reverend C. Hugh Hildesley. The church has been a remarkable example of dedicated service and inspiration for more than 66 years, nurturing the Carnegie Hill village.

Although Carnegie Hill's grid of identical rectangular blocks was formed as early as 1811, there were few settlers. This area remained quite rural, even abandoned, until the 1880s. By then the Indians had departed, poor scratch farmers loafed in isolated shanties and stark mansions had been built by brewery tycoons George Ehret, owner of the largest brewery in America, (at 94th and Park) and corpulent Jacob Ruppert (93rd and Fifth now 1115 Fifth Avenue). There were many hospitals, laundries and gloomy institutions, such as the New York Magdalen Asylum for "erring and indigent females" at Fifth Avenue and 88th Street. On 86th Street between Madison and Park Avenues was located the New York Christian Home for Intemperate Men.

Over the next thirty years, buildings were erected in architectural styles that came to typify different periods in the city's history. Carnegie Hill became somewhat fashionable. It was OK to live way "uptown." Meanwhile, developers took the opportunity to build 15-story apartment houses on Park and Fifth avenues; the top floor penthouses were designated for the servants of the patrons living comfortably below. Coming into vogue in the 1920's, these high-ceilinged luxury buildings, one or two apartments to a floor, were a more convenient abode than houses on the upper East Side boulevards. Yet for the most part, family-size houses of brownstone and limestone reigned on the side streets providing light and scale and human communication. The combination of small scale-houses and sweeping apartment buildings along the avenues of Carnegie Hill lent the community a distinctive eclectic air that has not been lost. The vital essence of the old village pattern remains.

The Indians who had occupied the northern portion of Manhattan Island, the "Manhattans," called it Manhatta, "hilly island." Underneath the pavement where we sledded and hopscotched had been the Indian village of Konaande Kongh, "the place near the sand"—referring to the sandy point that had extended along the mouth of the Harlem Creek into the East River. Here had stood the bark-covered residences of three score Weckquaesgek Indians.

Before the arrival of the Dutch, the "Manhattans" made a path west from East 96th Street to what is now Central Park that connected with the Manhattan Path running south to the bottom of the island, home to some of the Canarsie Indians. (Most of them lived in Brooklyn.) The Canarsie Indians sold Manhattan in 1624 to Peter Minuit for baubles sometimes valued at $24. There is no evidence that the sly Canarsies ever shared any of this largess with the Manhattan Indians on Carnegie Hill.

The Carnegie Hill Neighbors group, against virulent bureaucratic pessimism from city "experts," developed an enormous sustained program of beautification and harmony that makes a moment's walk through any part of the discrete area a joy.

Carnegie Hill has the unmistakable character of village living. Residents of the houses and apartment buildings stop to talk on the streets and in the shops. Community activities continue throughout the neighborhood, day and night. The 92nd Street YMHA has an outstanding program of literary forums, debates, concerts, lectures and art shows—an energetic village-style activity repeated in many places throughout Carnegie Hill. Signs of village pride are clearly visible: cohesiveness, concern for breaches of the peace, attention to public beauty, and environmental care. A fine healthy environment induces and sustains the congenial mood. There is little of the cold, indifferent atmosphere generally ascribed to the cities.

Personal safety from criminal assault and robbery is not guaranteed. But Carnegie Hill, like any village, is probably less subject to violence and mayhem than are other sections of the city. Carnegie Hill Neighbors provides, thanks to a healthy contribution by the neighbors, the extra safety measures of car patrols, guards and a doormen's surveillance and reporting system that utilizes cellular phones. Police from the 19th Precinct are known to respond to 911 in minutes.

What we may be experiencing now, when cities have grown too big, remote and dangerous, is a return to modes of living that were not only acceptable but necessary centuries ago. Villages once scorned, are perhaps returning to warm regard and satisfying primeval needs for a human scale, self-containment, friendship and beauty. Our biological evolutionary psychology is somehow satisfied in an unconscious yet compelling manner.

28.
Early Days on
Carnegie Hill

I walked to the top of the village on Carnegie Hill at 93rd Street and Park, just after Charles Lindbergh had flown thirty-three and a half hours solo to Paris and appeared as Man-of-the-Year on the cover of the new *Time* magazine.

It's a strange feeling to have lived on Carnegie Hill for more than half a century and to see the subtle changes along the avenues and side streets of this small village neighborhood. The staying put stimulates remembrances of early days and slows the rush of turbulent modern times.

Park Avenue, just a few years before my family arrived, was an open eyesore sewer of uncovered railroad tracks from which Commodore Cornelius Vanderbilt's locomotives belched soot and steam as coal-fed trains rattled north and south between thick granite tunnels. By 1927, the shanties, pigsties, saloons and breweries strewn in muddy squalor had been replaced by handsome townhouses. Elegant verdant center-island malls now covered the railroad cut, newly named "Park Avenue," stretching up imperiously from the new Grand Central Station Terminal.

The world of fashion was mesmerized by the transformation

from low scale to up scale, and a herd-like stampede of masters, matrons and mistresses began from Fifth and Madison avenues to Park.

My father purchased, with my mother's dowry, cooperative apartment 9B at 1172 Park Avenue, on the southwest corner of 93rd Street, across from financier George F. Baker's red brick Georgian mansion (now the cathedral center of the Greek Orthodox Church).

Each day the railroad hidden under Park Avenue carried more than 100,000 commuters in and out of the city. Day and at night, I heard poignant sounds from the tracks below of trains, now electrified, rattling, grinding and squeaking their way to and from Grand Central, two miles to the south. Today, I still live only a few yards from the Park Avenue railroad tracks, in constant earshot of the trains traveling to and fro. I don't regret the presumed indignity of a location near the railroad tracks, so downgraded in American literature, or of constantly hearing the clackety-clack of the railroad cars. In fact, the trains just below my window have become a kind of comfort, a companion of noise and thunder, as much a part of life as memory and family.

I remember the first fall day in 1927, refreshingly warm and smelling of hops (similar to the odor of burnt carrots), when the family, newly arrived from the Village of Babylon, Long Island, crossed the Park Avenue Rubicon. Afterward we walked across 93rd Street to Madison Avenue passing the Alamo apartments, which in 1945 became the locus of the film *The House on 92nd Street*. Then around the corner by the old pharmacy, now the Corner Book Store, which has retained the drug store's oak shelves for books. Then past Gristedes and the Wales Hotel, across to the 90th Street Pharmacy and over to Fifth Avenue. Then on to Central Park through the Engineer's Gate, where signs placed by

Parks Commissioner Newbold Morris said, inhospitably, "Keep Off the Grass." Morris lived in our apartment building and was deemed aloof, despite a reported friendship with Mayor Fiorello LaGuardia.

This was the golden age of the railroad. The grandeur and comfort of the financial barons' private cars has never been equalled. Both George F. Baker and Andrew Carnegie had private cars. Carnegie built his ultimate Georgian mansion on squatter's territory on Fifth Avenue. His private railroad car was parked under his resplendent quarters overlooking Central Park. It was a long way from his modest birth cottage in the village of Perth, Scotland, overlooking, I recall, the Perth River and two busy distilleries.

Across from Carnegie's mansion, to the south, a temporary tennis court was located on Fifth Avenue at 90th Street. The afternoon after we arrived on Carnegie Hill, my father, out of a mixture of kindness and frustration, took me on an afternoon walk through the neighborhood. As we approached the tennis court. we saw a large new sign that proclaimed: "On this Site will be built the Church of the Heavenly Rest (Episcopal)." My father pointed his cane at the sign. "See that," he said, raising his voice, "that's where *you* will be going to church—whether you like it or not." The church had purchased the valuable lot from Mrs. Carnegie for a million dollars on the condition that the new building's roof would be low enough to allow her sufficient sun on her own garden, to the north across 90th Street. The Heavenly Rest Church has no steeple.

Later that day my mother took me on one of her "errands"—to find little shops to feed a family of six. I remember going along Third Avenue where enormous elevated railroad trains roared by, deafening us for minutes afterward. Conversation would simply stop mid-sentence. We would resume, unperturbed, a few moments later.

At the corner of Third Avenue and 89th Street was a colorful fruit and vegetable stand (not unlike the Impressionist painting of a fruit stand by Gustav Caillebotte) manned by a man with coal-black eyes. Mike polished and sold the best, and we returned regularly to his stand under the El. He sold, both pink and white horseradish, which he ground fresh on the street, one hand amiably touching his cap.

We passed a stationery store on the way home. Its red sign said, "La Primadora." Mother stopped to enter a daily subscription to *The New York Herald Tribune,* which at that time featured Beatrix Potter's Peter Rabbit, stories which my mother read to me unfailingly and still bounce in my head. The owner of the shop, two steps down, was a friendly round man who became known to us as Mr. Epstein. He relished the subscription and the new family entering the neighborhood. He gave me as encouragement a penny chocolate and a big-boy pat on the shoulders. Eighteen years later, I returned on a furlough from the army and walked by Mr. Epstein's shop, now larger and on the other side of the street. There was a sign in the window written by hand in block letters: "This Shop Is Closed Today," it said, "one-half in Memory of the death of Mr. Epstein and one-half in Memory of the Death of our President, Franklin Delano Roosevelt."

In the 1920s women did not work and were known as house-wives except for those who were nurses, teachers or nuns. Being a housewife was no easy breeze. Mother was up at dawn and worked on a variety of scheduled chores until long after dark. She bought all the groceries and supplies herself in a round of little neighborhood stores whose merchants were glad for the business and gave anecdo-

tal good cheer and service when we entered their domains. I soon
learned that a housewife could secure a cut of beef more tender and
less costly if the proper relationship had been established with Joe,
the butcher. Joe said that he wore a wide-brimmed straw hat to keep
from getting colds in his head, running as he did back and forth into
his ice-cold refrigerator. He gained some notoriety in the neighborhood one day by asking Mrs. Wallman, who complained to him that
his chicken did not smell good, whether she herself could pass such
a test.

The trains below Park Avenue are noisier now, not unpleasantly
so but more defined, as if orchestrating a melody of all the years of
coming and going.

I think about first arriving at 93rd Street and Park, and I wondered what this neighborhood will bring to us next. Then the sounds
from the tracks come louder and louder—the click-click, the rumble, faster and faster—and then, as quickly, fading out, slowly, slowly,
until there is no sound except automobiles licking the melting snow
as they rise to make the big hill at 93rd and Park. Then I hear (I think
for the first time) the mordant sound of a train's horn—*whoooaaa* —
strange. Faint thunder now and a brisk rumble and cough as the
night deepens. Trains on the old railroad track below rush on to the
suburbs and beyond.

Carnegie Hill village, resilient and resonant, has stayed virtually
the same. But there are more flowers—tulips each spring and bego-
nias each summer and fall, annual beds and well-trimmed hedges—
more flowering trees, cleaner air, more schools, five major Fifth
Avenue museums—and more children. In a world of anomaly
Carnegie Hill has gotten better. One villager got it right, saying that
Carnegie Hill has the best of both worlds: "Here you can live in a
village a block or two from the city." As neighbor Suzanne Fox put

it, "America has far simpler neighborhoods—places built at a single time, planned in a single style, and settled by a single group of people. I, for one, am thankful that Carnegie Hill isn't one of them!"

Carnegie Hill is a phenomenon. As a whole it is blessed and well-cared for. It might give city planners some insights about what, after all, appeals to the soul.

29.

Scene of the Seasons from the Sixth Floor

Unlike a small village where I lived once in Hawaii while trying an overlong lawsuit, Carnegie Hill experiences distinct and welcome changes of season.

Constant, bland summer climate debilitates the spirit. The shifts to autumn, winter, spring and around again to summer, on the other hand, can be stimulating, even fascinating to observe minutely from the sixth floor, overlooking the sweeping center-island malls that run up Park Avenue from Grand Central. Undulating for visible miles until archly going up and over the heights at 93rd Street, these island malls of changing seasons then disappear into sunken rail tracks with crowded housing projects on each side.

The upper East Side around Carnegie Hill is curiously redolent with primary and secondary schools. Some of the children are so small that when a yellow bus picks them up along Park Avenue, you think it's a ghost vehicle, since you cannot see their heads through the windows. A child is escorted by a proctor to the bus door and, once inside, vanishes.

In this busy area on Carnegie Hill, invaded each morning by honking yellow buses, are the Spence School; Dalton schools, 89th and 91st; Saint Bernard's in the English tradition; Sacred Heart; Nightingale–Bamford; Saint David's School, where daughter Andrée is chief chef; the Day School Church of the Heavenly Rest; the Brick Church School across Park Avenue; farther south the gray-stoned Park Avenue Christian Day School and many more, dutifully handling a daily morning influx and early-afternoon exflux of little people.

The schooling is expensive, and it is serious. Perhaps, the biggest hurdle in the life of the affluent parent is getting little Hillary or Christopher into the right kindergarten. Hearts are broken if the child doesn't get accepted.

Before the ant-like array of yellow buses converge at 91st and Park around 8:00 A.M., honking-honking interminably (as if this frustration would speed the process of unloading the precious cargo), there's another poignant scene that we can observe from the sixth floor.

There—across Park, marching briskly, is a man with a trailing wool scarf. He holds a long leash attached to seventeen dogs that are trotting after him. All kinds of dogs. All sizes, colors, moods and dispositions: cocker spaniels, terriers, shepherds, collies, dalmations, bulldogs, Afghans, Great Danes, boxers and others. This incredible promenade is a regular feature of the avenue at about the time the yellow buses, yellow taxis, and station wagons descend on the cluster of schools. It seems that busy parents and children do not wish, in the hassle of getting to school on time, to walk their dogs in the inclement rush of the morning.

The dog man lets his entourage stop a moment across the street. Some of the dogs sit patiently; some do not. The man with the scarf is quick to pick up and dispose, avoiding an enforced $100-fine. The uniformed doormen at the apartment awnings are bored with the dogs and honking vehicles, ubiquitous every morning, but spring to the alert when a dweller wants a cab to go "downtown." A doorman blows his whistle. The harnessed dogs, as if alerted by a signal for them, march up the hill.

Green trucks arrive in the confusion of grid traffic to unload Christmas trees for the Park Avenue islands. Bright lights are delivered to dress them for the annual December illumination outside the Brick Church. By nightfall of that evening, the streets are filled with adults and children, the smallest ones on parents' shoulders, the better to see. Songs are sung, the festive lights go on, and many remember earlier days and maybe old dreams of living in the country.

Winter comes with ice and snow. In the 30s and 40s the snow used to be heavier, piling up along the curbs as high as one's head. Sledders and skiers to this day appear out of nowhere. Cars scream and whine trying to get up and over the icy hill at 93rd Street.

The wait for spring is worth it—especially in this city where the contrast of weather seems severe. The Carnegie Hill Neighborhood Association produces and maintains all the flowers and flowering trees along Park Avenue from 86th Street to 96th Street, while keeping the whole district safe, historic, beautiful. Like clockwork, the spring tulip bulbs go in. What colors will they be this year? Finally the tulips come up, triumphant, in the spring sunshine: butter yellow and pinkish red tulips around the salmon cherry trees. Birds will sing in the trees until summer, when the children happily vanish to camps and seashore.

Whether we live in the city—sometimes, the culture of concrete congestion—or not, I believe we cannot somehow forgo our primitive yearning for natural beauty and natural living. As the seasons revolve, we count on the intangible pleasures, so simple and so necessary, of dogs, children, Christmas trees and song, birds in the trees along the avenue, and the pink, red and yellow tulips, so visible and appreciated, from our sixth-floor apartment window. City living can be rewarding if we remember to engage it with the natural pleasures of the village. That may be the secret of true urban living.

30.

Ocean Village on Île de Saint-Barthélémy

There is a little tropical village, newly formed on an island with the lilting name of Île de Saint-Barthélémy on the Bay of Grand Cul-de-Sac in the French Antilles.

This village is gracefully dotted with small gumdrop houses built on diminutive hills, sheltered and infused with colorful splashes of bougainvillea, hibiscus, plumbago and laurel. The houses are horizontally wood-paneled and porched, have four-sided roofs painted the soft palette of pastels and, situated for privacy, and look out at the Caribbean and the Atlantic: The village is called Guanahani —far-off San Juan Island, first sighted by Christopher Columbus in 1492 in the misnamed West Indies.

The taste and style of France, 7,000 kilometers away, has created this exquisite place. The colors applied to interiors and exteriors are those of the island's flowers, the ocean and the sky. The accessories in the hotel naturally are Hermès; Porthauld, and vivid madras—exuberances of Manuel Canovas and chief designer Michel Jouannet. There are smooth, bleached arched cedar ceilings; white colonial fans; some rafters stained deep blue or deep green; and wide terraces of soft plank wood. But perhaps the most characteristic detail on the buildings of the village is the white-painted cornice of rick-rack, or, as it is sometimes called, gingerbread.

Possibly 6,000 years ago a volcano spewed the gigantic brown rocks and lava that created on this magic island the lofty platforms for gardens and terraces overlooking Grand Cul-de-Sac Bay. From on high we can seen an amazing protean phenomena of sea and sky and mysterious islands far offshore, beyond the pounding, cool mint waves.

Here is a village to savor and remember.

31.

Mougins
Idyllic Place du Village

Mougins, if you wish to find it, is hidden away nine kilometers north of Cannes in Provence, southern France. It is a village that rings a peak bearing a lookout. The circular eagle's nest, way up high, majestically overlooks the southeast coast of France and the brilliant blue Mediterranean. On top of the lookout is the Place du Village—the quintessence of Mougins village.

Here villagers of Gaul in the 11th, 12th, 13th and 14th centuries took turns, I imagine, looking south to the sea for evidence, any sign, that fierce, ingenious Moors or Philistines were invading this lush and attractive region. Should the villagers spot trouble below, the bread, wine and bouillabaisse would be put aside, and ancient alarms would be rung throughout the land, all the way to Lutetia, the place we call Paris. If the mauranders were judged overwhelming, the villagers, trained in vigilance for a thousand years, would flexibly yield ground and retreat northward with as many of their possessions and livestock as they could manage. On another day they would return to this blessed piece of heaven called Mougins.

Looking down on Mougins from an airplane, the village looks like a peeled blood orange—the thick skin of umber going round and round, providing access to the center. The central village rises as a mountain climbs. Dwellings hug each other, and the buildings on the outside of the orange have spectacular 360-degree views: the sparkling sea, the Maritime Alps, the lavendered valley of Grasse, plains and rising verdant hills to the North; and the new farms and dwellings to the east toward the bustling port of Nice. (The Nice International Airport, one of the prettiest in the world, has an attractive marble interior decorated with palm trees. The vibes are good, and it is no problem to pick up a rental Renault or Citroen.)

Once in memorable Mougins, you park on a natural lower garden level and amble up a small path as if aiming for a party at someone's estate in Greenwich. You find a tall square clock tower, thick old fortifications, handsome ancient houses, tiny cobbled streets, artists' shops and colorful small restaurants with white-hatted gourmet chefs ready to serve. Flowers in season and flowering trees abound. No humble window ledge is without a pot of primroses. There is no shove or push. There's no acrid commercial flavor or barker's bark. No one solicits or begs. You are soothed by the spirit and peace of this extraordinary place.

As you approach some tiny parks displaying small fountains, graceful sculptures and flowers, you notice how naturally Mougins has been contoured and how pleasant it is. You drift happily on to another opera setting, the Place de la Maire. Which restaurant? Which table outside in the sun and air? Which little passageway to explore the art galleries, flower shops, grocery stores and fortress caves, selling books, magazines and antiques?

The roofs are as ruffled as burnt almonds glistening in the sun. Vines of hot colors creep up and down. Balconies are everywhere with flowers flowing down to the street and pots of flowers—all neat, clean and beautiful. Privacy is assured inside the buildings, and coolness as well, by white-painted shutters that swing effortlessly open and closed.

While walking around the circumference of the central village, you note the peeking presence of the yellow-white stone clock tower, with its large encased bell ready to announce an invasion, or simply morning Mass. The poppies in the fields seem to be rushing up to the minuscule houses; the flocks of olive trees sing in the breeze of ancient days of daring, sweet chivalry and energetic trade.

Below the upper village of Mougins is a series of wider circles of houses, other buildings and more houses, each with vegetable and flower gardens. These expanding rings of living provide a playground for the rich, the famous and the retired. The entire district of Mougins (village and environs) makes Mougins, in its entirety, one of the largest villages in France. But you have to be told this on good authority, because the eye is so gentled by the human scale of the place, the naturalness of the landscape, the curve of the footpath and the light and the flowers. The French have a knack for and an irre-sistible pride in seeing to it that each scene is attractive, neat and harmonious against the contours of the village, sky and sea.

The embracing cluster of the old stone houses, with their tiers of luteous rooftops, seems affectionate. We want to stay here. We want to come back.

In 1961, in New York, Alexandra's first interior-design boss sent her as a young intern to David Findlay's gallery to view some paintings by a new French artist for a client in New Orleans. For the first time Alexandra, fresh out of the New York School of Interior Design, looked at this artist's work.

She was so overcome by the beauty and color of Roger Mühl's

paintings that her heart pounded and her spirit was moved. She spoke to Findlay about her enthusiasm, which he shared as well. When recently in Provence, he had told Mühl: "I truly like your artistic work. You are a genius with your eye and your brush..."

Alexandra, in the excitement of her own discovery, took her mother out to lunch that day and told her she had become enamored of the impressionistic figures and landscapes, painted in extraordinary light, by Roger Mühl—a French Alsatian artist living with his wife, Line, in Grasse, a perfume village just north of Mougins.

Alexandra's mother was somehow persuaded to put up the money, and a Mühl painting was selected, framed and delivered to Alexandra's apartment—34 years ago. This was the start of Alexandra's collection of the paintings of this masterful artist. Over the years, she and I and Brooke have fortunately become friends with Roger Mühl and his family.

When the Mühls chose to move near to the Place du Village in Mougins, we were introduced to this sublime village. Every year we go back once or twice or even three times. If you are tired of Mougins, you are tired of life.

Roger and Line Mühl, who have always kept absolute privacy, bought an ancient, handsome stone house. Once you are inside, you overlook the glories of the valley and the green, purple and yellow hues of the Maritime Alps from several tiers of terraces, enveloped in stunning and well-kept seclusion. A stairway of stone on the inner north wing leads to Roger Mühl's sanctum studio.

The incomparable surroundings, the tincture of the flowers in garden, village and valley, imprint Mühl's retina. Then the flow of his artistic magic creates paintings of light and color that give happiness and inspiration to everyone who possesses his art. His paintings are now found in Germany, Japan, Switzerland, Italy, and throughout the United States and Canada.

It is surely significant that Picasso chose to come to Mougins toward the end of his life, to appreciate the colors, natural beauty, favorable climate and serene atmosphere. For we know that Picasso, at that stage, had many locations in the world from which to choose to live and paint and die. He chose Mougins.

When Napoleon was first exiled at Elba, he succeeded in escaping from captivity and marched back to war for 100 days (only to be curtailed by Waterloo) up the Napoleon Road, right past a fine restaurant and inn, formerly an old olive mill, called Moulin du Mougins. It is still in operation: here are eight little suites over a superior restaurant whose owner-chef, off and on, is handsome, white-moustached Roger Vergé. Vergé and Roger Mühl of course are friends. When Alexandra and I go back, time and again, we notice that Vergé has placed more beautiful Mühl paintings of Mougins environs throughout the Moulin du Mougins restaurant and the cozy, paneled white plaster bar.

Another oasis in this paradise is the new Hotel de Mougins— four Provençal buildings surrounding a large garden and pool. Your rented car can take you from there on your own day trips to the canary yellow Colombre d'Or restaurant and inn in the ancient walled village of Saint Paul de Vence, then to Matisse's chapel near-by with his exquisite, colorful cut-out windows. On to elegant Cannes with a whiff of Hollywood and to old-time Nice and the joys of Saint Jean on Cap Ferrat; on to Cap Antibes where the F. Scott Fitzgeralds and the Murphys played and fought; and, if you have sufficient gas, francs and tolerance, on to Monte Carlo.

But above all the greatest human pleasures of soft beauty and inimitable village life may be found, without hassle or turmoil, in sweet Mougins. Nearby, the artist Roger Mühl paints its glories.

32.

Paradisal Village
The Phoenix
Rise of Eel Island

Once upon a time there was a tiny island plunked down in the sparkling, azure northern Caribbean Sea: shaped like an eel, heading west—fifteen miles long, two miles wide. Flat, drought-dry, no mountains, no natives (the Arawak Indians are no more; they did not eat the Caribs), no hotels, no telephones, no off-load piers, no television, no shopping malls, no political parties, no self-government, no secondary education, no electricity or running water. But with lots of free sun; grand views of other islands, with majestic purple and green mountains and bays; the finest white sand beaches in all the world; and the friendliest, most competent, independent local inhabitants you can imagine, descendants of Africans who never were slaves.

In the late '80s and early '90s, a miraculous transformation took place that made Eel Island (whispered to be a British colony) a garden of Eden—as yet not fully discovered by earth tourists who fly in and out on bird airplanes.

A delightful newly created village of several hundred souls rose out of dreary scrub and desert on the peaceful west end, surrounded by the roaring sea, designed and planned for a decade by enlightened entrepreneurs. The founders knew and understood history, particularly tumultuous Caribbean history with its mercurial weather (as recently as 1966 Hurricane Donna stripped the island bare). Other islands had been created by the violence of volcanic eruption, but serene Eel Island rose from the accumulation of corals centuries ago.

The prescient developers acquired the most modern technology and created inspired architecture stunningly suited to village site, although plainly not indigenous to the region. Today, the white Moroccan villas appear to have always been here, sublime since ancient days.

With a rare appreciation of natural offerings available here of beauty, the deep cerulean sky painted as if daily by an imaginative artist, the developers pursue their dream. They profit, too, from experience culled from enormous research into the tribulations of similar village and resort experiments, near and far. Additionally, they apparently know finance, so the enterprise should not falter, or slide back unhappily to where it was a few solar years ago.

Food, wine and rum are imported to the village, where chefs, trained we imagine in Perigord, conjure dishes long remembered for their subtlety and flair. Local lobster is as succulent as that enjoyed anywhere in Canada, on Maine islands such as colorful Monhegan, or at Block Island, Montauk, or Stonington Village. These lobsters display plump white meat of extraordinary flavor, and can be savored with an inexpensive Louis Latour Chardonnay 1993 Andrèche from northwest of Avignon (where Stone Age art 20,000 years old was discovered recently). The executive chef playfully produces the best varieties of culinary delight, enhancing the timeless formula of fresh meats, poultry, seafood and—a key elusive measure—beautiful greens and vegetables: baby carrots and onions, flowers of broccoli, shaved cabbage, tiny asparagus, small peas, tasty tomato slices, tender leaf spinach and nosegays of cauliflower.

Eel Island is a masterpiece appreciated most, I think, if you come to it from such cacophonous, odoriferous urban centers of jangled nerves and ill pollutions as Caracas, Bombay, Karachi, São Paulo, Los Angeles and New York. You feel right away the contrasting, elevating muse, the soothing antidote to what is euphemistically called civilization. After a few days you begin to become a different person. You literally relax. You put things off. You refuse to fax, compute or telephone. You start to live again. You literally enthuse.

The village fathers, while not omniscient, are intelligent in their administration. The first thing they built was a desalination plant, camouflaged but definitely necessary; now ample clean water spouts from the spigots. The botanical crews proudly learn, nurture, plant, water and care for thousands of flowers, bushes, flowering trees, towering palms, ferns, cacti and bay grapes galore; the flora is so dense and colorful as to tint our retina for a long time.

The extraordinary light permeates our visual system and regulates each body's interior clock. We sleep better lulled by the rythmic pounding surf. We awake to a bright blue sky and the gentle knock of those good and cheerful souls who bring us breakfast and a new day.

The birds respond to this evolution of beauty by appearing regularly in costumes of brilliant yellow against black—flitting, turning, darting, nibbling the sugar and the jam. They twit more than they sing, but there is time.

Eel Island has seduced us for additional reasons having to do with the wisdom of the village's creators. Their accomplishments have sensibly reduced our dismay with any village that is not strictly 18th century or antediluvian.

The Eel Island newly-created community village,★ constructed from shrub and sand, today provides the seamlessly essential attributes for living well: beauty, security, caring people, necessary services, healthy food, special effects such as inspiring architecture, sugar beaches, green oceans and coves for swimming and sailing. Best of all, visitor and resident find privacy, that precious serenity that is disintegrating all around us as the millennium turns.

★Cap Juluca, Anguilla, W.I. Keep the secret.

33.

Giverny
Claude Monet's
Normandy Village

A particularly sublime village in France is Giverny, where for many years Claude Monet gardened and painted. One sunny October day, Alexandra and I set out from Paris for this magical place, following the Seine all the way with our van driver, Paul, who amiably revealed to us his enthusiastic grasp of the mystery and grandeur surrounding Giverny—and its most famous resident.

Claude Monet is worthy of exaltation because of his persever-ance in painting beauty in Giverny in his own medium of color and light. Like no other man, he created his own environment around him—within his walking distance. He did this carefully day to day, season to season. He saw, contemplated, renovated. Giverny was his own natural palette. His artistic subjects fell back behind his brush strokes of sunlight and shade, black against yellow; pink, rose, blue, white, orange, purple.

He made his great alert house, tudored and narrowly rectangular, a glow of pink by applying crushed brick. He chose natural green for the door, shutters, porch and outdoor furniture. The house is a sentinel standing with dignity and watching over the village land-scape to the Seine.

Monet had an uneasy life, drifting between towns and villages, mostly along the Seine. His paintings, in gradation, reflect these places, some of which he deplored. (Monet may have irritably destroyed more of his paintings than he kept.) He thrilled to a beautiful environment and was miserable where mediocrity was urged and prevailed. So it was with great joy, while riding on the little local railway between Vernon (across the Seine) and Gernay, that he spied, at the door of the train, the little Norman village of Giverny. Some say he then spotted the house that he eventually bought for 70,000 francs. He felt instantly that Giverny was the place for a permanent home for himself, his family, his paintings and his gardens.

Monet's beloved Camille died of tuberculosis in 1879, leaving two sons, Jean and Michel. The Monets and the Hoschede family had been friends. After Alice Hoschede's husband, a prominent mer-chant and art collector, went bankrupt and fled to Belgium, Alice decided to raise Claude Monet's children along with her own. Eventually they moved, together as one family, to Giverny, where Claude and Alice remained until the end of their lives. The village was then, and is today, idyllic: a Norman church steeple, green rolling hillsides overlooking a strong river, embankments of flowers and flowering trees. The river Seine figured prominently in Monet's life. When he was a young man working near the river in a paint shop, he met the artist Eugene Boudin, who urged him to go along to the wide sandy beaches of Le Havre and Trouville to paint the passing scene in the open air. Some romantics say this was the beginning of the Impressionist movement. In 1872, in fact, he did exhibit a paint-ing which he had entitled "Impression, Soleil Levant." Traditional uptight critics found Monet's loosely fashioned canvases, brushed intuitively with brilliant colors straight out of the tube, reflecting nature and light, to be undisciplined if not repulsive. They called Monet and his coterie of itinerant outdoor artists "the Impressionists."

Yet Claude Monet was always a serious artist in earnest pursuit of new ways of releasing beauty, light and dimension. His house at Giverny, his garden, his flower-banked pond, creeks and streams became his studio. Like a divinity, he created his own spirit of place, suitable to his temperament, perfected to his eye and agreeable to his muse.

As his success increased exponentially, Monet put more and more time and resources into the design of his burgeoning paradise. He purchased adjacent land and diverted the small river Epte to form a lovely moving pond whose soft currents flowed on into the widening Seine, then on to Le Havre and the Atlantic where he had started painting with Boudin.

Monet constructed greenhouses and built barn studios for his large canvases, to be studied and worked on in changing light. He developed his vegetable and fruit gardens. He never stinted on his breakfast of hot chocolate, fruit and pastry, or on elaborate lunches or dinners, for he loved good food and good wine as much as beauty. Slowly, he conjured a sublime world around him on the graceful hillside outside the village. From the early 1880s until his death on a cold December day in 1926, Claude Monet lived a full and mostly contented life in his peaceful kingdom, surrounded, but not suffocated, by family and friends.

After Monet's death, his second son, Michel, inherited the property. Through the years, there was no longer the same attention to detail. The gardens became overgrown, the plants were neglected and the house and studios rotted in the wet climate. When Michel died in 1966 after being injured in an automoble accident, the entire property under his will went to a responsible recipient, the Académie des Beaux-Arts.

In 1977 Gerald Van Der Kemp was appointed curator of the Monet Giverny property. This was a fortuitous choice. He quickly took charge of what became a major accomplishment: splendid and honest restoration of Claude Monet's home and gardens as a living museum. He and his wife, president of the Versaille Foundation, developed ingenious methods of raising substantial funds in Europe and in America to accomplish an authentic and tasteful recreation of the way Giverny used to be when one of the world's greatest painters did his magic there.

For visitors from all over the world, the revitalization to the original state is breathtaking. Now we know, or think we can surmise, the extraordinary source of Monet's inspiration. From this selected site of less than two and a half acres, the celebrated genius created a microcosm of rare beauty. And a skilled, talented curator wins the international prize for restoration of a remarkable phenomenon.

We can imagine Monet, walking along his garden paths with a cigarette and hat, buttoned-up wool jacket, old sweater over his shoulder, white beard on robust chest. The creek burbles under the Japanese bridge, painted his color of French periwinkle blue, and on to the miraculous pond that he wrested, despite bureaucratic obstacles, from an ugly dry gully. Monet stops to brush mauve wisteria from his shoulder and once again contemplates his water lilies, his searching eyes interpreting the vertical nature of a horizontal scene. He feels the interplay of water, vines, color and light—exploding and imploding, shimmering quintessence of exquisite beauty, delightful gems floating on air and on water: "Nympheas," out of the soul of Claude Monet.

At Giverny we feel the presence not of the apparent peasant with the refined mind, but of the magnificent artist who introduced us to modern art, and incidentally, to where and how to live.

PART FIVE

I

When I see the past, what I see are not just the failures of human effort, of human imagination, but that unquenchable desire to make of life a meaningful thing.

ANTHROPOLOGIST DAVID FREIDEL

II

Never leave your village when your garden is in bloom.

JACK LENOR LARSEN

III

I am a part of all that I have met.

ALFRED, LORD TENNYSON
ULYSSES

IV

In the final analysis our most common link is that we all inhabit this small planet. We all breathe the same air. We all cherish our children's future. And we are all mortal.

JOHN F. KENNEDY

V

Perhaps my best years are gone…but I wouldn't want them back. Not with the fire in me now.

—SAMUEL BECKETT
(found on pub wall in Coronada, California)

34.

The Headline Says, "Quality of Life in New York City Declines"

A responsible newspaper survey headlined not long ago that most residents of New York City believe the quality of life in the city has declined. While this report may not be earthshaking, it is interesting to notice the critical areas that the harassed city dweller feels contribute to this ominous malaise. A majority of those polled had a grim view of current and future city life because they were convinced that the city was less safe, the economy bad, race relations poor and the public school system in shambles.

"In its most provocative finding," *The New York Times* reported matter-of-factly, "the survey determined that 45 percent of the respondents said things had gotten so bad in New York that they would move out tomorrow if they could. Some pollsters played down the significance of the finding, noting that similar surveys in Chicago and London also showed many residents said they wanted to leave immediately."

"'I wish I had the money to get out of the city," said Joanne Walter, 34, who lives in Cobble Hill, Brooklyn, and has three children. "There are people going through the garbage. There was a hooker on my corner the other morning. They broke into my car several times. My mother was mugged. It's rough.'"

Quality-of-life—in these terms—spoken as one word, became the central issue in the New York mayoral election that year and served to elect Rudolph Giuliani, Republican-Liberal, former ace federal prosecutor. The poll indicated that depressed city residents, pounded by hard times and a bad environment, were not persuaded that either the incumbent at the time, David Dinkins, or his challenger could alleviate the decline of the city quality of life.

"The city has gone down," said Nan Babiak, 27, as reported by the *Times*. She lives in Williamsburg, Brooklyn. "I've noticed a lot more crime on the street. If it could get any dirtier, it looks like it has."

The *Times* presented a more recent poll on April 18, 1995, that showed two-thirds of the New York region's residents are less than satisfied with the quality of life. It also found that forty-two percent of the people living in the New York area would move out tomorrow if they had the opportunity. Again, in all regions, crime was identified by nearly one in four people—regardless of age, race or economic status—"as the single factor most affecting the quality of life."

Op-ed columnist and *Times* journalist A. M. Rosenthal has the quality of life in New York City on his mind. A long-time city resident, he is a valiant observer of what's going on. His columns are pungent and his influence is great. I wrote Rosenthal a year or so ago to express a view that, before all else, the first right, the first freedom, in a civilized society is to be able to walk about one's neighborhood in safety and without fear. Alexandra and I had recently been brutally mugged a block from our apartment at 90th Street and

Park. I enclosed my written account of the episode and my hope that he would write forcefully about this issue that is, we think, acutely poisoning the city. People have been fleeing in droves for more than forty years.

What I delivered to A. M. Rosenthal was a true story of the misery of becoming prey, day and night, to pathological assaulters—young psychologically deprived raiders who roam the city streets determined to kill and maim, if necessary, in their urge to loot and mug and rob. And there is increasing evidence in myriad reported cases that more and more of these predators are shooting and stabbing defenseless victims *after* they have acquired their illicit bounty. In your face, they say. These young and not so young male bandits are often strangely devoid of compassion and conscience.

Here's what I sent along to Rosenthal:

A fragile lady crossing Park Avenue in New York City at 92nd Street on Carnegie Hill, January 10, was mugged and killed by assailants riding in a van. She was grabbed by the head and shoulders and dragged along the street until one of the rear wheels of the van squashed her head like a melon, leaving blood and her dentures in a deathly crimson stream across the avenue. She had carried her purse by a strap slung across a shoulder and was on her way to lunch with her sister across the street.

The peaceful Carnegie Hill village neighborhood had been victimized by a series of vicious muggings in recent months—the latest by a pattern mugger on a bicycle who attacked, one at a time, six elderly women.

Memories of the Central Park "wilding" nearby, bringing rape, robbery and near death to a young female jogger, had made Carnegie Hill residents uneasy, but now a *killing* for a purse in *broad daylight* in the middle of Park Avenue on top of the highest

Manhattan hill induced some alarm. For the next few days the streets below our apartment windows were empty. Two days later, two policemen patrolled between 93rd and 90th streets on Park, with their billies, the first such security measure I'd seen since the days of reform and Mayor Fiorello LaGuardia.

At 9:15 on a clear summer Sunday night in 1989 my wife and I were attacked and robbed by two strangers, a thousand yards from our apartment on Carnegie Hill. (The killing of a woman by the moving van purse-grab took place, in broad daylight, at 92nd Street and Park Avenue, also about a thousand yards from our apartment.)

We had finished supper at a small umbrellaed café, around the corner, and were returning home on the left side of 91st Street, walking arm and arm in the cool night air, by the primary Dalton School, and toward the Brick Church. No one was visible in front of us.

Suddenly, like the explosion of a land mine, from over a low wall, flashed a crushing blow to my head and neck.

The lightning impact of the karate blow, by heel of a boot, lifted me from the sidewalk and sent me flying into the middle of the street. As I hit the tar, I looked up to see two assailants surrounding my wife, punching her, yanking at her chain-purse over her right shoulder and pulling at a gold bracelet and green strapped watch on her left wrist.

I found myself yelling so loud that for days afterward I could hardly talk. As I got to my feet, the attackers—one tall, the other short and wiry—ran east toward Park Avenue.

My wife was close to hysteria as, in the eerie amber street lights, we watched the muggers clear the Park Avenue mall and rush down toward Lexington Avenue. They had ripped off the purse and the watch. They departed as suddenly as they had appeared. Five or six men, women and children returning from visits elsewhere immediately answered our shouts for help. A small posse of neighbors (including the doorman from 1130 Park Avenue) then chased the robbers down the hill, toward Lexington Avenue.

Meanwhile, a woman put her head out the window to exchange exclamations with the small gathering below. "I already dialed 911," she shouted.

Police and undercover detectives came in seconds as if they'd been casing the usually quiet neighborhood. They asked, notebook in hand, about a car that had been driven in hot pursuit of the attackers *east* on 91st Street—a *westbound* crossroad! The courageous driver was Richard Bernstein, a reporter for *The New York Times.*

One of the breathless chasers returned to tell us, standing dazed on the corner, that they had caught one of the two at 91st Street and Third Avenue. Would we come down and identify? In a few minutes we found the shorter partner-in-crime sullenly glowering and hissing, baring teeth like a caged wolf.

The impact of his karate blow had ripped the buttons off my jacket and left me in trauma and pain. I now realize that the karate blow had been aimed at my head and in the flash of the attack I had instinctively put up my left hand for protection like a besieged boxer. My wrist and arm took the force of the blow, casting me headlong into the street. (The next day x-rays showed three fractures of the left hand.)

Alexandra, feeling the blows to her face and body and the savage violation of her spirit, stood among some forty people now gathered around the captured mugger.

A police car backed in and detectives lifted the resisting captive into the back of the car where handcuffs were snapped on him. The assaulter then bizarrely proceeded to engage in a series of frenzied convoluted Houdini tactics to squirm out of the handcuffs. Detectives subdued him and drove him off for booking for assault, battery and robbery. He was the 175th *arrested* mugger in our 19th Precinct in the last eight-month period.

After indictment by a Grand Jury, he pleaded guilty to all

counts, benefited by plea bargain tolerance and liberal judicial compassion. He was sentenced to a year in jail. His buddy was not apprehended, although twice a member of the family came over from Brooklyn to demand more money from me. The second time I called the detectives from the 19th Precinct, who responded quickly. Two of the detectives deftly arrested him and took him away in handcuffs because he had Alexandra's purse in his possession, having offered it to me for a cash payment.

We have observed tragic brutal attacks on our neighbors. One person, Stephen Petchek, was shot in his face by his assailant after being robbed. Our Rector, Alanson Houghton, had a gun put to his temple—on 93rd Street and Madison Avenue—as he was relieved of some of his worldly goods.

Recently, a slight lady was on her way home at Fifth Avenue and 93rd Street when she was hit on the head from behind as she carried her groceries, and while prostrate in the street, robbed on a sunny afternoon.

Alexandra and I remember with dreadful sadness discussing one evening with a mother the killing with a golf club of the woman's daughter by a robber who ambushed her from the bushes of Central Park while she was riding the bicycle given to her that morning on her sixteenth birthday.

What has gone wrong? America has always prided itself on dedication to liberty. Most Americans came here from other lands to secure liberty—the crown of any civilization.

Without liberty we live in servitude. The crucial element of freedom is not academic rhetoric and Fourth of July fireworks. The key to freedom is the assurance of *personal safety,* for our families and for our neighbors.

Basic freedom should mean the ability to move about one's community without fear of being maimed, robbed, and killed. We cannot live a life cooped up in an apartment as if serving behind bars a sentence for wrongdoing.

We must, at the least, be free to visit the neighborhood grocer, our place of worship, the pharmacy, the book store, our neighborhood café. To be chased to and fro so near our home is unacceptable, no matter how righteous sociologists and pundits explain and debate the sociological and biological complexities and the increasing turbulence of modern life.

The current onslaught against the personal safety of the average citizen seems to worsen month after month in urban areas across America. There seems no escape from this insidious cancer eating away at the basic quality of life.

That was my message to columnist A. B. Rosenthal.

Happiness may well be a state of mind, but the quality of life in your neighborhood can make an enormous difference.

Mr. Rosenthal never has responded to my account, but the other day he did sum up the city's dilemma quite well:

"This is the world's most exciting and creative city; the others are vanilla. But it is suffering from a civil, moral and political disease that can kill it dead. It is called [borrowing Senator Daniel Moynihan's telling phrase] 'defining deviancy down.'"

35

Despite Lack of Safety and Other Troubles, the Vision of the City Set on the Hill Persists

In early 1995, New York City Mayor Rudolph W. Giuliani gave a cautiously upbeat speech at the Yale Law School, proposing a New Urban Agenda.

His vision for New York City, and similar American cities, was a reincarnation of the eternal dream of the City Set on the Hill—although poetic metaphor may not be the mayor's forte.

"The continuing success of America as a great nation, depends in large part on the future of our cities, as growing and thriving centers of innovation, creativity," he said earnestly. "The cultivation and development of our culture and civilization largely happen in our cities."

His prospective was not to perceive and complain about "their problems," which he concedes exist in spades, but rather to concentrate on cities as vibrant "assets" making large creative and cultural contributions to city citizens, the nation and the globe.

The Mayor's rallying theme is worthy of consideration: when America and its cities faltered socially and economically in the despond of the Great Depression, the population had substantially shifted off the farms and villages to the cities. Conditions were insufferably bad. Simply surviving the crisis was so severe that the federal government in the early 30s assumed a mandate to direct and control the roles that had been granted to the states and the cities within them. This social engineering revolution directed out of Washington, D.C., continued with populist force through the 1960s under President Lyndon Baines Johnson's Great Society.

Thomas Jefferson in early days recognized the pull and tug of urban policy direction between centralization and decentralization in self-rule. Jefferson, a wise reflective man, often spoke of this dilemma: "When we direct from Washington when to sow and when to reap, we should soon want for bread."

As a people, we tend to move more by experience than by theory. The French observer Alexis de Tocqueville, echoed by Emerson, wrote of the ceaseless American struggle between the conflicting natural impulses of communitarianism and individualism.

President Franklin Delano Roosevelt was persuaded by his brain trust and British economist John Maynard Keynes to jettison the old policy (which followed Say's Law of markets, i.e., that production drove consumption) and that the way out of the Depression was to trigger demand by government spending, thereby encouraging consumerism.

Mayor Giuliani, in his seminal address at Yale, urged the cities and states to take back control of the cities' destiny and let the federal government attend to its traditional duties and responsibilites—national concerns of war and peace, national domestic prosperity and the general welfare.

The mayor interestingly envisioned Paris as a model of his ideal. Foreign governments such as France view their cities, he suggested, as part of the national treasury.

"In France, Paris is the hub of the nation's economy. The French government understands that Paris is a prime sight for international investment and that the city is a generator of wealth, a spectacular tourist attraction, and the possessor of the heart and soul of what makes France the great nation that it is."

(France is still the only nation on the globe that requires the study of philosophy in high school. A lesson there.)

The mayor was direct if not tough. He told his New Haven audience that the federal government must not only return responsibility and cost functions to the cities to solve their urban problems but also return to the cities (and the states) the financial resources that the mammoth federal government has been siphoning down to Washington, D.C., for some two-thirds of the 20th century. He pointed out that the widely held belief that the federal government supports cities is "precisely the opposite" of the truth.

For example, he said, "The City of New York and the State of New York send to Washington, D.C., fourteen billion dollars more than is returned by Washington, D.C., to the city and the state. Eight to nine billion dollars of that emanates from the city of New York. Now, the state of Georgia, receives one billion dollars more than it sends to Washington, D.C."

Mayor Giuliani was elected Mayor largely on the belief that he could address the pervasive levels of crime that were driving people out of the city. It is refreshing to hear him tell his audience that he thoroughly recognized the crime problem "that it is our responsibility, not the responsibility of the federal government." On his agenda he puts "public safety" first. This is a huge change. After that, more jobs, and education and other urban-oriented responsibilities to improve the quality of life.

The mayor told with enthusiasm about similar innovations and a concentration of leadership focus in other American cities such as Philadelphia, Chicago and Los Angeles. "Very similar things in these cities are being turned around."—The awakening maybe of the cities?

He ended his energetic speech by citing Saint Augustine's maxim, *Omnia civitis, corpus est*—Every city is a living body. The audience appreciated the mayor's translation and appeared impressed yet perhaps, being academic, assumed a posture of wait to see more concrete results, the awful distress of the cities being so long and so intractible. But the problems have now been addressed without guile or cant and the debate may continue in evident sincerity.

36.

Slab Architecture and the Banalities of Bad Zoning Contributed to the Decline of New York City

Before World War II, New York City perhaps had a last chance to develop more neighborly communities, more of the human-scale, diverse districts and enclaves that tend to give the resident as well as the visitor a smile of happiness.

There was then a certain equipoise between the insistence of such autocratic city planners as Robert Moses that the city should be a *showplace,* a super-grand metropolis that would look good on film, and the more humane view of Jane Jacobs (expressed in her fine 1961 book *The Death and Life of Great American Cities*) that skewed Grand Plans for the city as horror scripts; she, to much derision by highbrow critics, advocated "order in variety" and the "ballet of the street." Jane Jacobs, a feisty lady who lived in and loved to be in Greenwich Village, within the city, largely and sadly lost out in the battle for the city's future aesthetic direction.

At the height of the high-flown debate in the 1950s and 1960s,

I believe that the general public, that is, the non-experts, were not sufficiently informed, or consulted about, the somewhat esoteric issues and arcane rhetoric used by the leading proponents, such as Grand Official Planners (Moses), city life stylists and village-loving theorists espousing city-friendly ideas (Jacobs).

One beneficent exception was Mayor John V. Lindsay, who, many believe, saw the true picture and its consequences and did everything he could to lift the important priority of making the city a better place to live, against the inexorable grandiose tide of pseudoscience, of "bulldoze" planning—e.g., the loss of magnificent Pennsylvania Station and the collapse of traditional small-scale street architecture.

Most city dwellers seemed unaware for the most part that the struggle for human-scale zoning and aesthetic preservation of historic places was going on or that the outcome would affect, in any significant way, the real quality of their lives. We have learned too late.

The winning trend to Grand Metropolitan Megalopolis was exalted mostly by architects, planners and politicians in other American cities, so the impact of the New York City debacle became a sad-city syndrome nationally.

In a 1,374-page book published in 1995, *New York 1960,* architect Robert A. M. Stern and two colleague historians shed some light on this New York City debate and picked the bones of its consequent developments. Now ordinary citizens, some of whom have fled, can see what was happening then and the fundamentally unrewarding results.

Particularly telling are the authors' description of the city's repeal of the "pioneering zoning ordinance of 1916," which had maximized ground density and "opened the city skyward" with salutary "set back" rules. The Grand Plan developers, some lobbying with force and cash, reversed that light-air-human-proportion formula, encouraging "unmodulated, independently spaced skyscraper slabs ..." New zoning introduced tower skyscrapers to the east-west side streets, further blocking light, air and sun and magnifying, and somehow celebrating, mass density like a black urban umbrella. The whole unfortunate, if not greedy, process may account in part for what is characterized by the authors as the loss of "the camaraderie of street and neighborhood life, so long the glue that kept the city's social fabric together."

This chilling, pushy incremental procedure cast a pall on the desirable village attributes of city life as we used to know it. Into the void stepped not inertia, but hostile antisocial behavior, graffiti, gang warfare, drugs, robberies, car jackings, rapes in the parks and even apartment buildings, muggings and murders around the clock sufficient to raise the fear that the city streets have been taken over by enemy forces up to no good.

Slab architecture and the banalities of bad zoning cannot be held solely responsible for the decline of the ambience of New York City and similar mega-cities. But their contribution to it has been sufficiently severe to warrant placing blame where it belongs and to look with hope toward essential reform someday.

37.

Soothing Serenity
of the Village

René Dubos told a story about how King Charles I in 1635 summoned an Englishman, Thomas Parr, to London to honor him for attaining the age of 152 years. Old Parr, as he was affectionately called, hurried up to the City of London, where he was celebrated, wined and dined in an endless outpouring of congratulations and awe. In the midst of this intense conviviality, Old Parr died.

The renowned surgeon William Harvey performed an autopsy and reported that Parr's organs were, despite his age, in good shape— indeed, "as healthy as the day he was born." Dubos said that Harvey attributed Old Parr's death to a surfeit of food and wine, and to the pollution of London's air.

In the winter of 1995, Alexandra and I traveled to Chicago, where her beloved, surviving brother, Powell Johns, was to undergo, at 57, a triple-by-pass heart operation and a second procedure to open up a major artery to his brain. Hours before surgery was to proceed, Powell, a cerebral type-A advertising executive, experienced dreaded numbness and tingling up his right arm. The surgeons told us that the risk of disability was about five percent.

We spent the evening before the operation with Powell in his room at Northwestern Memorial Hospital. He was in good spirits, laced perhaps with some melancholy and mystery. He had written letters to innumerable family members and friends, some of which arrived long after he died.

While competent surgeons worked hard and successfully on the intricate heart by-pass procedure, Powell suffered a massive stroke, paralyzing his right side. During the next three days the crisis intensified, and he drifted into a deep coma.

The family gathered. The waiting room was crowded with sad, anxious relatives and friends confounded by the modern technicalities, uncertainties and the confusion.

Alexandra was in the midst of the turmoil day and night. The doctors and the chaplains consulted endlesly, earnestly, with family members. The trauma was penetrating, and there was no relief.

Without having regained consciousness, on the fifth day Powell was given last rites and extreme unction by an Episcopal priest who suddenly appeared as if on cue in a small play. The family were all there around the bed, touching the body on which Barbara, a devoted intensive care nurse, had placed a box of tissues.

Everyone was exhausted. All the tubes were removed, and Powell was summarily pronounced dead by the doctors. We were perplexed by the surge of medical events, the rush and roar of the disaster centered on one we loved. Death is never really known until it's met on intimate terms, like being hit by a truck as you cross the street.

Hours later, Alexandra received a telephone call from a good and wise friend who is an able surgeon in Jackson, Mississippi. He is also an esthete—a poet with a real love of beauty and serenity. He lives in hospitals but, with his wife, Mary Ann, carefully planned and built a Georgian house overlooking a lake where swans choose to live. Dr. Petro had been following the ordeal from a distance. Now that Powell was dead, he had some advice for deeply distraught Alexandra.

"Go to the village," he said. "Go as soon as you can to Stonington Village to restore, recoup and recharge. What you need," he suggested gently, "is the healing power of nature: The village environment promises, as it always has, the keys to health and well-being." He reminded her that, biologically, we are the same as prehistoric man.

"We strain and stress in an overloaded technical environment. We should all return, if we can, to the natural state, the serene atmosphere of the village."

The next morning Alexandra said to me, "Come on. We're going to the village. I know the doctor's prescription is right."

And it was.

38.

Granville
Transplanted Village

Granville in Massachusetts and Granville in Ohio are twin examples of the secondary migration of a village. What salient factors caused entire families in the early days of the 19th century to transport themselves to the vagaries and sacrifices of the wilderness?

The first Granville, in the foothills of the Berkshires, was one of the prosperous, well-populated villages of eastern Massachusetts. Organized in 1754, the village extended to the deep gorge of the Farmington River, 12 miles to the west. But the people of Granville suffered, along with other New England villages, the turmoil of the Indian Wars and four years of Revolutionary War resistance to the British as well as divisive religious controversies. The people in Westfield, Springfield and Granby, Connecticut were friends and neighbors. Hartford, the big city of the region, was down an easy road just thirty miles away.

At the end of the 18th century, a majority of the people in Granville made the sometimes painful decision to migrate to the far-away Western Reserve in Ohio. The economy of the village was rapidly declining. The cause was, incredibly, overpopulation. In 1765 there were fewer than 683 persons. In 1790—the year of the first

Federal Census—there were over 334 families totaling 1,979 persons. By the tilt-point period of 1800, the population reached 2,309—more than Springfield. One half of this population were under sixteen years of age. In just 34 years the population had tripled. This was an apex of population for Granville. (Today there are about 1,000 residents.) The farming simply did not provide enough food to feed so many mouths.

Additionally, by 1800 the thin glacial soil had been overworked to a point of less return. The land around Granville was simply exhausted. The village leaders intelligently recognized an approaching crisis. The remedy was clear: a large migration westward, to be executed in a series for convenience and safety.

In March, 1805, after extensive and anxious preparation, a body of twelve villagers set out in ox carts and wagons, crossed the Hudson River and followed a route known as the Pennsylvania Turnpike. The speed of the journey was the speed of the ox. They reached the site that would become Granville, Ohio, a month later and immediately planted corn for feeding the next, larger group. The second group built a sawmill and erected cabins. Then came surveyors and administrators. The site, now laid out, was named Granville: With its high hills, it looked and felt just like Granville, Massachusetts.

Granville, Ohio, developed rapidly and well because an intelligent, cohesive leadership group planned the village with skill and care. Soon girded by strong New England traditions, it had a library, a sound responsive local government and—a church with a fully developed schism…Successful schools and colleges flourished in this environment. The Young Ladies Institute blossomed under Baptist authority. It eventually became amalgamated with well-regarded Denison University, previously the Granville Literary and

Theological Institution. That institution had been founded in 1831 by the pioneering Denison family of Stonington, Connecticut.

For many years the chairman of Denison University's board of trustees was John E. F. Wood, a Rhodes scholar and an able senior-law firm mentor of mine. He would say, "Yes, Denison is not big like Harvard, but it is unique because of its resistance to secularization and its adherence to the importance of the spiritual growth of its students." And then, looking me in the eye: "Smaller can do that better." I believe he was right.

Granville, Ohio, with its New England houses on its hillsides, is lovely. It remains for all to see and confirm a striking example of a New England village transplanted.

39.

Notes on the City of Paris
The Best—Why?

Paris—the very word enchants. This is Saturday in mid-February, not a touristy time; the weather is crisp, the sun bright and dappling. We're at a small hotel, Le Duc de Saint Simon, on the Left Bank. Room No. #22 is minuscule—perfect. The care taken in decor, color and constraint is admirable.

We are in a cul-de-sac tucked away from bustle and traffic, up Rue Saint Simon; we are, in effect, in a small village. The inhabitants, the shopkeepers, the people walking by, exude a *nowness,* the importance of being here, at this moment in this blue, heavenly, sunlit time.

We step off narrow sidewalks to allow parents and babies to go by. Even in the less architecturally recognized areas of Paris, there is nonetheless the inescapable elan (chic!) of other, more elegant areas.

How is it that Paris—through foreign invasions, wars, riots, communal uprisings and other catastrophes—has maintained the exquisite beauty and clarity so satisfying to the souls of both visitors and to lifelong residents? Its resonance burnishes all those who are here.

Paris has always been a circle of delight, appealing to all human beings, whatever age or inclination. First, the light. In appreciation of any place, there is no substitute for the presence of light. Few people spend time wondering how the extraordinary light comes about; they are content simply to absorb its sublime pleasure. The light makes Paris gregarious. People sit outside at cafés (such as Les Deux Magots, 6, Place Saint-Germain-des-Prés) all year round, and sometimes all day. Sound studies have confirmed the vital significance of light on personal health and well-being.

Paris is a round landscape bisected by the wide and lovely river Seine, flowing directly through the city, winding gracefully around two gemlike islands and then wending on, majestically, to the Atlantic Ocean. On the way, it nudges briefly such enclaves as Giverny.

It is always Valentine's Day in Paris. Restaurants are booked—brasseries, bistros, intimate places with blue, purple and red faces, fancy formal places such as Ritz-Espadon on Place Vendôme, with the phallic monument to victory and glory. Once ensconced to dine, no one hurries. Madonna and her rock, jacket-less boyfriend wait impatiently outside. (Restaurants in Paris are for dogs, too, large and small, well behaved. The big ones disappear under the table. A bone is produced out of a Chanel handbag.) Wine loosens tongues and lilts conversation, and cigarette smoke rises, providing a mysterious haze of romance. Women, consciously, dress attractively. No $100-sneakers. Men hold hands with ladies across white tablecloths past crystal wine glasses. Candles are lit at dusk. Couples kiss on the street, repeating their good-byes.

The design of the city of Paris is ingenious, more for beauty than for defense, and it heightens the esprit of the soul. You are literally glad to be alive here, to see the triumphant sweep of the boulevards; Greek, Roman and Norman buildings, in all directions; apartment houses and plane trees etched by artists; and diminutive circular parks with cobblestone streets curving around to show more architectural splendors. Allées of sturdy green foliage everywhere. Clean fountains spray pure water. Walk around Paris before you die.

Traveling at any time from the Left Bank to the Right Bank, or from Right to Left, confirms the magnificent panoramic documentation that this is the most attractive city in the world. Good people in green uniforms, using green brooms, keep it clean. Flowers are planted all around in the winter—primroses, pansies and daffodils galore—and even in gentle rain or under a skimmed milk sky, birds sing.

Parisians have somehow captured the capacious essence of living well in a broad urban environment. There is no feeling of the incontinent mega-city. Its scale has human beings in mind. Skyscrapers rise up, but at a distance. We spy the Eiffel Tower to orient our journey on foot.

Paris is open and generous to its residents and welcoming to visitors from all over the world. It gives freely its beauty and symmetry and art—both to the rich and to the poor. The joys of this great city are shared; the consequence is a palpable mood of exhilaration and sensual energy.

The atmosphere of Paris is a bell ringing and flags flying, and we want to rejoice.

40.
Rural Village of Keane, Virginia
Journey To "The Old Rectory" on the Thomas Jefferson Monticello Road

One springtime, half a century ago, I drove along the Monticello Road, Route 20, through undulating rural meadows southeast from red-bricked Charlottesville, Virginia, to a small village-hamlet called Keane.

My father and mother had decided to retire from the rising tensions of New York City and the hectic pace of the New York Stock Exchange, to live—too late—in harmony in the yesterday village of Keane, a bucolic, idyllic place set amid spacious horse farms and plantations such as Lenox, Plain Dealing and Estouteville, and up the pike, the inimitable Monticello, designed with love by Thomas Jefferson.

Growing tired of their search, my parents discovered one day in 1941 no Palladian farm-estate, but rather something within their possibilities: a small white-clapboarded, green-shuttered house called, since the early 19th century, The Old Rectory. Here had resided for many years the impecunious Episcopal minister of small Christ Church only a few hundred yards, what is still today a dirt road. A diagnosis of terminal cancer caused my father to return to New York, and my parent's dream of living in Keane was never realized.

There are no other houses in view from The Old Rectory; instead, looping miles of wooden white-washed fences, the greenest grass, shiny brown and chestnut gray horses. The Rectory itself is encased by boxwoods, fruit trees, flower and vegetable gardens and a few stark outbuildings. The approach is a gracious, circular pebbled driveway and four flagstone steps to a diminutive porch with two slim doric columns (a nod to Albemarle County architecture). A solid black-green door is centered with a thick brass knocker that is deeply engraved, "The Old Rectory."

All this sweet serenity on a few acres; an outpost perhaps, for a regal part of the world made known by the creative splendors of Thomas Jefferson, James Madison ("Montpelior") and James Monroe. Meriwether Lewis, William Clark and George Rogers Clark, sons of Albemarle's pioneer families. The golden age of this area probably peaked from 1785 to 1850.

Nowadays, this blessed unspoiled landscape is resting somewhat on its laurels. What surprised me the most as we abruptly came upon the village of Keane for the second time, in November 1993, passed the insular Green Mountain Store (and gas station), turned left a quarter-mile later to take the dirt road to Christ Church and glimpsed The Old Rectory through the boxwood and white picket fence—was that, in half a century, nothing—*nothing*—had changed.

Here was an unworldly rural village setting in Albemarle County that was frozen in time, even more than Nantucket and Stonington

Village, Connecticut. The Keane general store, the neighboring horse farms, Plain Dealing and Lenox, The Old Rectory itself, Christ Church and the road to old Scott's Ferry on the James River (Scottsville) were just as they had always been. On the grand hills on each side of the road, a sense of repose and dignity enveloped the traveler as if to say, this is the way it was when local men such as Thomas Jefferson, James Monroe and James Madison were presidents of the United States—good enough—and this is the way it is now. With this time warp perspective, I suspected that industrial progress and urbananity may be overrated.

The opportunity to return to Keane after so long a time had been provided by Alexandra's popularity as a lecturer and author. She had been invited by a Charlottesville bookstore and the Junior League to give two lectures. The bookstore owners, Allan and Cyndra Van Clief, lent us a large car and invited us to come to Christ Church in the southeast countryside for Sunday services.

Driving out to Keane that day with Alexandra, I felt an eerie sense of time's passage and a certain retrospection—perhaps as the pre-war butler did venturing down rural English roads in the book and film *The Remains of the Day*.

We had careful driving instructions from Allan to the isolated church off the Thomas Jefferson Road and did not expect to pass The Old Rectory. Therefore I experienced a mysterious feeling of déjà vu when I saw the house to the left, with an identifying sign in black on a white stake. As we went by, turning right onto our instructed dirt road, I found myself foolishly saying to Alexandra, "You know, that house on the left was The Old Rectory. I was there once in 1941." She smiled, replying, "Yes, I know. That was the year I was born."

We parked our car along the church driveway and looked

around. A large hill rose in the sunlight across the road. A score of black- and brown-spotted cows lay lazily on the thick green carpet of the hillside. Not a sound. The cows were acting their part in a 19th-century landscape painting.

Christ Church is set on a gentle crown of land, with amazing command for a perfect little brick, square, gable-roofed building, another Albemarle gem of architectural design. Its white pews with chocolate-brown trim are open in the democratic tradition. There are large 16-pane windows on both sides, a neat oval pulpit, a graceful altar rail, and a small baptismal font behind which a diminutive organ, played that day with gusto and lively simultaneous vocal accompaniment by an enthusiastic volunteer. "When the congregation is small, I sing louder," she said.

Choir member Joey Haeckel heard from us the saga of The Old Rectory. She skipped into the vestry room to telephone current owners (since 1960) Colonel and Mrs. Robert Ranlet. Joey Haeckel returned, whispering to me, "Mrs. Ranlet is on the phone and would like to talk to you." In the vestry room, I spoke for the first time with Mrs. Ranlet. She came to the point:

"I understand that you are at Christ Church and are interested in the history of our house. Will you be here long?"

"No," I said, "we'll be returning to New York Tuesday after Alexandra lectures in Charlottesville tomorrow." I then repeated my memory of my first visit to the house and the unexpected pleasure of coming upon it that morning.

Mrs. Ranlet had heard enough and said, "Well, when can you come over?" To which I replied "How about now, for a few moments? We're on our way to Monticello."

I was excited about revisiting the old house after so long a time. Perhaps the return was made more poignant because of parents' long-sought dream never came to be—the poignancy of what might have been.

Here it was. We stood at the green door. I rang the bell. No answer. I gripped and wrapped the shiny brass knocker. The door slowly opened and a man said, "I am Mr. Ranlet. Please come in." We introduced ouselves. Mrs. Ranlet joined us. I found myself talking in the hall about my parents' buying the house in the early 1940s. Mr. Ranlet looked quizzical, touching his ear. *"Couldn't have happened,"* he exclaimed, a small smile. *"We've lived here forever!"*

Mrs. Ranlet graciously urged us into the living room, to the left of the front door, a lovely comfortable room, full of Jefferson's basic formula: light and air. Here was an attractive center fireplace and a white wood mantel of the Golden Age period. We sat and chatted.

Finally, Mrs. Ranlet said, "I suppose you would like to see the house." She rose and led us to the south porch, which she had artistically fashioned into a flower and plant conservatory. We then visited the library across the hall—again cheerful, well lighted, lined with books and displaying a portrait of Mr. Ranlet as a colonel in World War II. He had subsequently spent three years in Morocco performing special government service. The Ranlet's extensive travels were reflected in the personality of the house, which now, after 33 years of residence, was all theirs. An easel in the study, turned to the clear east light, showed instantly Mrs. Ranlet's artistic talent. She had been, we later learned, a leader in the world of artistic publishing.

When I awkwardly mentioned that my parents had restored the house but never moved in, the colonel seemed to glower a bit. "Nonsense," he gruffed, almost inaudibly. "*We* did the restoration." That was that, and I let it go. How nice for Alexandra and me to be guests in this old house that had lived so long somewhat dormant in my memory.

We said our good-byes to the Ranlets and returned to the car for the short trip down the road to Monticello.

Back on the Monticello Road, we again were fascinated by the extraordinary rustic scenery: high rolling green hills and swooping white fences, brown four-banded fences, roaming horses, lumpy cows, lost sheep, red barns, white barns and fertile fields rising from innumerable rivers—the rivers receiving water from the lush pastures, ridges and gullies.

These Albemarle County roads offer a historic legacy of scenes and stories to the traveler, for Albemarle's architects   guided our young country, surveyed this fertile terrain, acquired the acreage and, for good reason, settled here for generations.

Unlike roads north and west of Charlottesville, this area quietly offers the past at its best: crests of the magnificent Blue Ridge Mountains, quaint bridges, apple and grain mills, general stores with wood stoves, picturesque villages, tiny hamlets, farms as far as the eye can see, and taverns serving ale and cornbread.

Our car swung us up the little mountain to Monticello. It was by coincidence the 250th anniversary of the birth of Thomas Jefferson, philosopher and leader of the American experiment. Alexandra and I walked together toward the great house he designed himself. Jefferson, like his house, is universal, a symbol of the high ideals of his words and deeds. As we entered, we felt the light and the air, the symmetry and the comfort. This is where he wanted to be, where he always wanted to live.

I thought back to The Old Rectory in Keane, the first visit in 1941 and then the recent one. There was much to ponder in this sublime environment of Albemarle County and Thomas Jefferson country. The scale and symmetry were right; once again I felt the spirit of place. I couldn't help thinking of Stonington Village. Alexandra said she had the thought—a realization of what is appropriate and beautiful for a specific time and place.

What makes life transcendent and exciting is finding the right place to live and to learn how to live.

Letter to the Reader

I learned this, at least, by my experiment: that if one advances confidently in the direction of his dreams, and endeavors to live the life he has imagined, he will meet with a success unexpected in common hours…If you have built castles in the air, your work need not be lost; that is where they should be. Now put the foundations under them.

HENRY DAVID THOREAU,
WALDEN

VILLAGE—just the word—evokes varied responses depending on the mental picture of our own personal experience. In these sketches I have compared and contrasted the benefits and shortcomings of the village with the city as they may directly affect our lives in the coming new millennium. The subject and the choice are more crucial when we reflect on the few days we all have left.

Whether to choose the village or the city, or someplace in between, is a deeply personal decision, and the debate continues around the globe. The very idea of leaving the city is a recent concept of the past half century.

For more than 9,000 years, men and women have dreamed not so much of the blessings of their ancestral village but rather, obsessively and with heady excitement, of an adventure at the City Set on the Hill. (As Frank Sinatra would sing, if you can make it there, you can make it anywhere. He wants to wake up as a big shot in the city that never sleeps. Each to his own.)

Upwardly mobile, emigrating villagers are as stubborn as salmon returning upstream. Their perseverance in fleeing to the city may be strengthened by their attitude toward their village: its seeming dearth of opportunities, lack of bright lights and culture, the hard ceaseless labor; also perhaps their awareness that villagers have long been characterized as slow, old-fashioned, behind the times and villainous. Escape to an exciting city environment would provide the cultural amenities (art, theater, music, lyceums, restaurants, medical centers, welfare) and a chance to "succeed" and make one's way to a "better life," and best of all, be more free to pursue illusive happiness.

That these goals are vague and ephemeral in no way has appeared to lessen the frantic drive to quit the village and scramble up to the golden City Set on the Hill. The tide was somewhat reduced after World War II, however, when city congestion and new prosperity made the old Village newly attractive.

As many people still live in villages as in metropolitan areas. The majority of them—particularly in the Third World—are eager to leave and to travel to the city, regardless of the feedback about the desperate life and awful conditions in Rio de Janeiro, Jakarta, Bombay, Karachi, Cairo, Tokyo, Caracas, Hong Kong, New York, Chicago and Los Angeles.

Villages exist in the world as more than photographic shots on colorful travel posters. To survive, villages must be an economic unit, usually with agriculture or fishing, sustaining itself on the sale of surplus to people in the city or the suburbs, or where most Americans, caught between the dichotomy of City and Village, choose or are compelled to live.

The three million villages of this planet are not, despite the mythology, in danger of extinction. Villages for untold generations have been the world's oldest and most durable social institution.

They emerged like shade grass, from 13,000 to 8,000 B.C. in the Mesopotamia region between the lush irrigated plains of the Tigris and Euphrates rivers. Ironically, there, in modern Iraq, the nightly fireworks of the Persian Gulf War took place, and there, in this bizarre nuclear world, village life might have ended.

Some evidence of even earlier villages, propped up like wheat stalks along the blue Nile in Egypt, is emerging. A visit there stunned us with the revelation that in some ancient villages not much has changed in thirteen millennia. On the road from Alexandria to Cairo, we watched patient oxen doing the irrigation, walking round and round. We observed in Asia, as if in another world, the isolated farms in the New Territory, adjacent to Hong Kong, and the primeval raising of ducks and pigs while fertilizing rice and vegetables with night soil. Along the road, a farmer walked resolutely to market, miles away, carrying a cylindrical hand-woven basket out of the top of which we saw a live pig, its eyes open.

Change for change's sake, we can assume, is not a vaunted attribute of the village soul. Change is more the slogan of the city, of a nation under siege or at war, under economic or social distress of apocalypse and dread anomie.

Mega-cities such as Cairo, in Egypt, and Baghdad, on the Tigris, no longer have room for new villagers with stars in their eyes and hungry babies, pleading to get in. These migrants are shunted to settle atop garbage heaps; most do not get beyond the smoky clangorous railroad depot that brought them to their hearts' desire. Here they may be forced to pay a day's wage or beg for a space on the rail terminal floor for their weary hacking bodies, their children strewn about them.

The second most popular word in the Bible is "city." Even Heaven is described in enticing terms as a City Set on the Hill. Why the constant yearning for the city? For most, the current reason is the harsh economic necessity to find food and job.

There is, I think, also a desire, deeply imbedded in the primitive brain, to go up the ladder of success, with joyful expectation, to a metropolitan community that promises to provide comfortable facilities as well as opportunity for families—the catalyst ingredient of hope.

The enticing sacred city will offer, they believe, housing, food, water, storage facilities, community, entertainment, health, medicine, romance, commerce, temples of the deities, wise literate leaders who can inspire and precious libraries, scrolls and books storing ancient memories and wisdom. Here the restless villagers hope, endlessly hope, to find a blessed, secure place of final destination—a life with some significance, with some happiness.

The legend of the extraordinary benefits for those who reach the City Set on the Hill dies hard, despite Dickens' London of Oliver Twist and the actuality of New York City, where a million people are on welfare—many born in slums with generational redundancy or recent arrivals from stricken villages overseas. Poverty is the parent of crime and revolution, Aristotle said before the time of Christ. The tragedy is that this desperate condition becomes entrenched and the cycle of poverty and despair goes on.

In ancient times, the city was by nature a fortress. The enemy was on the outside. Security—personal security—for each inhabitant, each family of the city, was assured as an understood and honored social contract. Of all benefits, security was the prize. If you could locate and be allowed to live in the city, you could have safety. Without personal security, other benefits and opportunities for advancement, no matter how attractive, were meaningless.

Security is the essential condition of human existence that has been lost in cities. It is a sad fact that, in the opinion of some, the secure expansion and legendary glories of cities, as envisaged in earlier days, have reached a turning point.

We have reached the paradigm of dispersal, for those who can afford to go, to the countryside. In the Middle Ages, villagers would decide the stench of the garbage pit was too much, and the whole village would move away. Now there are other equally compelling reasons for finding a new abode and having the nerve and resource to move.

In New York City today, for example, there is no true freedom to walk about in your own neighborhood. Of all the talk about entitlements, the freedom to move about in one's own community should be number one. Supposedly, some new statistics show decline of crime—robberies, muggings, rapes. But for city dwellers the perception of crime and violence persists even in so-called "safe" neighborhoods.

City dwellers try to learn ways and means to avert the mugger, killer, burglar, looter, robber, rioter, rapist—by street-smart strategies and nimble footwork—but the fact remains that daily criminal violence against the innocent in urbia as well as suburbia is now at a level of conscious fear unacceptable in a supposedly civilized society. In addition to local predators, sinister global terrorists now have acquired cheap means to destroy hundreds of thousands of innocent citizens at morning rush hour.

The social contract of assuring personal security to the city dweller was, I submit, materially breached in the last generation and shows little sign of recovery in the near future. Most signals point to continued severe difficulties of safety and traditional freedom lying ahead. This is the reluctant view of observers who are not running for state or national office or appointment to sinecure in a city bureaucracy. Most are silent and, if anything, vote with their feet to places outside the combat zone of gang wars, car thefts and the generous crossfire of stray bullets.

There is no question that the greatest sufferers of this downgrading phenomena are the poor people arriving in cities from villages to the south, the needy Caribbeans, Mexicans, Central and South Americans and from Asia. Even counting all our new immigrants—legal and illegal—America has only 5 percent of the world population. The complex problems of the cities mount daily, impacting on the moral and social fabric of the United States as a whole.

The evil discomforts of major American cities, such as New York, have already caused significant exodus—if not flight—primarily since the 1950s, mostly to suburbia. We must face these penetrating problems and honestly consider some resolutions that may serve us all a better life of living well into the next century. Simply accumulating material wealth without such resolutions leads to chaos and to oblivion.

Suburbia has been touted for years as the ideal *compromise* for living the beautiful life. But the suburban areas have caught city infections and malaise; they are exhibiting the deathly viral symptoms that drove city emigrants out in the first place to the pseudo-green and passivity of the suburbs.

A growing body of critics have pounced on the swift trend in America toward closed-off, gated village communities, from Seattle to Maine: They claim these communities are undemocratic, elite, cold to the spirit of the surrounding communities, cities and suburbs—that they turn their backs on outside problems of poverty, crime and environmental decay. Nevertheless, 32 million Americans have opted for the private, heavily regulated walled village. The trend is expected to double to more than 60 million persons in the next ten years alone. This phenomenon is driven by the honest desire for personal safety, predictability and control over people's own lives.

This is not, I think, a sly scheme to exclude people on the basis of race and religion. The United States Supreme Court ruled that out absolutely long ago.

Perhaps it is ironic that the earliest Cities Set on the Hill 5,000 years ago were walled fortresses assuring their citizens personal security. Because cities recently have failed to offer safety, it is not surprising that some mobile Homo sapiens have devised lawful ways to provide a safe and environmentally nurturing place for themselves and their families. But nonetheless, it is the theme of this book that the village of our dreams can and should occur *naturally,* without gates and walls around a cocoon.

Those who are fortunate enough to have a chance to choose what to do with remaining days on earth can seriously consider where and how they wish to live. There are no sure choices, no perfect places. Economics and propinquity (family, friends and place) play a hard constraining role. Three moves are equal to a fire, Ben Franklin observed as Poor Richard.

But assuming a reasonably fair opportunity to select and move at some point in our lives and the means to do so, perhaps the way to go might be back to the humane, human-scale, civilized environment of the oldest source of culture, aspiration and love—the natural village. It is the message of this book that the village, carefully and realistically selected, can offer us the greatest potential for living well, and aided by available new personal technology, a suitable, biologically satisfying, way of life in peace and in joy, for ourselves and our families.

The village, properly chosen in its own time frame, is a veritable metaphor for living well—and happily—in the years ahead.

Our search for our own village may be worth pursuing.

Time is short.

AUTHOR

Peter Megargee Brown, a practicing counsellor-at-law and a former Federal prosecutor of organized crime, is the author of four previous books. He lectures nationally on vital subjects affecting our lives today. For many years he has observed firsthand hundreds of villages and cities throughout the world, as vividly revealed in the intimate essays of *Village*. He is married to Alexandra Stoddard; they live on Carnegie Hill in New York City and in Stonington Village, Connecticut.